LOVE DIVINE AND UNFAILING

THE GOSPEL ACCORDING TO
THE OLD TESTAMENT

A series of studies on the lives of Old Testament characters, written for laypeople and pastors, and designed to encourage Christ-centered reading, teaching, and preaching of the Old Testament

IAIN M. DUGUID
Series Editor

After God's Own Heart, by Mark J. Boda
Crying Out for Vindication, by David R. Jackson
Faith in the Face of Apostasy, by Raymond B. Dillard
From Bondage to Liberty, by Anthony T. Selvaggio
From Famine to Fullness, by Dean R. Ulrich
Hope in the Midst of a Hostile World, by George M. Schwab
Immanuel in Our Place, by Tremper Longman III
Inconspicuous Providence, by Bryan Gregory
A Journey to Wholeness, by Mark Belz
Living in the Gap between Promise and Reality, by Iain M. Duguid
Living in the Grip of Relentless Grace, by Iain M. Duguid
Living in the Light of Inextinguishable Hope, by Iain M. Duguid and Matthew P. Harmon
Love Divine and Unfailing, by Michael P. V. Barrett
Recovering Eden, by Zack Eswine
Right In Their Own Eyes, by George M. Schwab
Salvation through Judgment and Mercy, by Bryan D. Estelle
Severe Compassion, by Gregory D. Cook

LOVE DIVINE AND UNFAILING

THE GOSPEL ACCORDING TO HOSEA

MICHAEL P. V. BARRETT

P&R
PUBLISHING
P.O. BOX 817 • PHILLIPSBURG • NEW JERSEY 08865-0817

Printed in the United States of America

Library of Congress Cataloging-in-Publication Data

Barrett, Michael P. V., 1949–
Love divine and unfailing : the Gospel according to Hosea / Michael P.V. Barrett.
p. cm. — (The Gospel according to the Old Testament)
Includes bibliographical references (p.) and index.
ISBN 978-1-59638-075-2 (pbk.)
1. Bible. O.T. Hosea—Criticism, interpretation, etc. I. Title.
BS1565.52.B37 2008
224'.606—dc22

2008033666

To Sandra Ann
My wife
Ever faithful—never Gomer

CONTENTS

FOREWORD

The New Testament is in the Old concealed;
the Old Testament is in the New revealed.
—Augustine

Concerning this salvation, the prophets, who spoke of the grace that was to come to you, searched intently and with the greatest care, trying to find out the time and circumstances to which the Spirit of Christ in them was pointing when he predicted the sufferings of Christ and the glories that would follow. It was revealed to them that they were not serving themselves but you, when they spoke of the things that have now been told you by those who have preached the gospel to you by the Holy Spirit sent from heaven. Even angels long to look into these things. (1 Peter 1:10–12)

"In addition, some of our women amazed us. They went to the tomb early this morning but didn't find his body. They came and told us that they had seen a vision of angels, who said he was alive. Then some of our companions went to the tomb and found it just as the women had said, but him they did not see." He said to them, "How foolish you are, and how slow of heart to believe all that the prophets have spoken! Did not the Christ have to suffer these things and then enter his glory?" And beginning with Moses and all the Prophets, he explained to them

> what was said in all the Scriptures concerning himself. (Luke 24:22–27)

The prophets searched. Angels longed to see. And the disciples didn't understand. But Moses, the prophets, and all the Old Testament Scriptures had spoken about it—that Jesus would come, suffer, and then be glorified. God began to tell a story in the Old Testament, the ending of which the audience eagerly anticipated. But the Old Testament audience was left hanging. The plot was laid out but the climax was delayed. The unfinished story begged an ending. In Christ, God has provided the climax to the Old Testament story. Jesus did not arrive unannounced; His coming was declared *in advance* in the Old Testament, not just in explicit prophecies of the Messiah but by means of the stories of all of the events, characters, and circumstances in the Old Testament. God was telling a larger, overarching, unified story. From the account of creation in Genesis to the final stories of the return from exile, God progressively unfolded His plan of salvation. And the Old Testament account of that plan always pointed in some way to Christ.

AIMS OF THIS SERIES

The Gospel According to the Old Testament Series is committed to the proposition that the Bible, both Old and New Testaments, is a unified revelation of God, and that its thematic unity is found in Christ. The individual books of the Old Testament exhibit diverse genres, styles, and individual theologies, but tying them all together is the constant foreshadowing of, and pointing forward to, Christ. Believing in the fundamentally christocentric nature of the Old Testament, as well as the New Testament, we offer this series of studies in the Old Testament with the following aims:

- to lay out the pervasiveness of the revelation of Christ in the Old Testament
- to promote a Christ-centered reading of the Old Testament
- to encourage Christ-centered preaching and teaching from the Old Testament

To this end, the volumes in this series are written for pastors and laypeople, not scholars.

While such a series could take a number of different shapes, we have decided, in most cases, to focus individual volumes on Old Testament figures—people—rather than books or themes. Some books, of course, will receive major attention in connection with their authors or main characters (e.g., Daniel or Isaiah). Also, certain themes will be emphasized in connection with particular figures.

It is our hope and prayer that this series will revive interest in and study of the Old Testament as readers recognize that the Old Testament points forward to Jesus Christ.

Tremper Longman III
J. Alan Groves

ACKNOWLEDGMENTS

Admittedly, I am responsible before God for what I have written, but I am indebted to many. I remember the first time I was confronted with the intricacies and difficulties of Hosea's prophecy—my first Hebrew exegesis class. My professor, Allan Brown, was completing his dissertation on Hosea's theology; the message of the book consumed him and consequently us in the class as well. That was many years ago, and although my interpretations differ some from his, I thank him for his contagious zeal for the message of this prophet. In working on this project, I looked again at his dissertation, and it generated fond memories.

I want to thank Eric Anest of P&R for his initial suggestion to me to submit a proposal for the Gospel According to the Old Testament series and for his work as the supervisor of the project. I express my gratitude as well to Tremper Longman III for his willingness to accept my proposal to write about Hosea for the series and for his insightful comments and suggestions at various stages of the process. He forced nothing, but his constant reminder that this is my book was pressure enough. It was a pleasure to work with him. I give my thanks to all at P&R for their willingness to publish this work and for their support during the entire project. Special thanks go to Caren Silvester. She and I have worked on several projects together, and I salute her for her editorial skills. She knows how to make me sound like me—only better. I should also thank the adult Sunday school class of Faith Free Presbyterian Church for listening to my thoughts about Hosea week after week. They heard either a synopsis of what I had just written or a preview of what I planned to write during the next week. Many said they were blessed, and I can only take them at their word.

I also owe a debt of gratitude to Geneva Reformed Seminary and Faith Free Presbyterian Church for the ministry opportunities afforded to me, including time to write. It is impossible to say how much my association with the Free Presbyterian Church of North America has shaped my ministry under God for over thirty years.

Of course, I must thank my wife Sandra for her constant support. Every morning she prayed that the Lord would help me to write, and every evening she asked if He did. She was always the first to read a finished chapter and always said, "Good job, Michael." Whether that is true or not is beside the point. She has been a constant source of support, not just during this project, but for most of my life. Thanks to Sandra, I know nothing of what Hosea experienced with Gomer.

INTRODUCTION

The tension between doctrine and experience is common in the Christian life. What we believe and know as fact doesn't always match up with what is happening in our lives. Objective truth often conflicts with subjective experience. More often than not our experience becomes more credible than our doctrine, and this creates the tension in our hearts. This tension extends even to the Scripture, which is the source of everything we believe and the rule of everything we are to do. We believe the Bible is God's Word. We believe that it is a living Word that is "powerful, and sharper than any two-edged sword" (Heb. 4:12). But notwithstanding that confession of faith, Christians far too frequently read the Bible and get nothing from it. Apart from a few familiar stories or a few favorite verses, the majority of the Bible, even for believers, seems irrelevant. Few know anything of what David experienced when he confessed God's Word to be more desired than gold and sweeter than honey and the honeycomb (Ps. 19:10).

This disconnect between confession and experience regarding Scripture is nowhere more evident than in the Old Testament. For various reasons, the Old Testament is a closed book for many Christians today. There is something about the Old Testament that corresponds to Peter's assessment of Paul's epistles as containing some things hard to understand (2 Peter 3:16). From Genesis to Malachi, the reader encounters hard sayings, obscure details, unfamiliar and enigmatic expressions, forgotten customs, family trees with unpronounceable names, and detailed laws that have no immediately discernible application or relevance to modern life. Much of the Old Testament seems to have no apparent value or purpose, and much seems to be outdated both theologically and culturally. The Old Testament provides a lot of hard reading without a lot of blessing—or so it seems.

Frustrations with the Old Testament often drive Bible readers to more familiar and more obviously devotional texts. Familiar and devotional texts are good, but when believers ignore the Old Testament, they are ignoring the majority of God's revelation and missing the blessing of finding nuggets of truth that are just as vital for modern Christians as they were for Old Testament saints. Indeed, that God's Word is compared to silver and hidden treasure suggests that the prize is not always lying on the surface. Part of the problem in most Bible study is that unless the message is on the surface, the average reader moves on in his reading, kicking up dust until coming across an obvious surface lesson. Shuffling along does not typically result in discovered treasures; sometimes we have to dig. Proverbs 2 says that if we seek truth as silver and search for it as hidden treasure, we will not be disappointed, for the Lord promises to give wisdom, knowledge, and understanding. Even the digging becomes profitable and enjoyable when we realize we are handling the very Word of God—the Word without which we cannot survive. From Genesis to Malachi to Revelation, the Word of God reveals changeless and eternal truth. We should keep our Bibles open and not give up until we discover the truth, because we know that God rewards those who diligently seek Him. He promises that when we seek Him with all our heart, we will find Him (Jer. 29:13). That is the truth.

The Bible says that all Scripture is inspired and profitable (2 Tim. 3:16). Faith believes it to be true. Faith in the inspiration of Scripture affirms the Bible's authority, infallibility, sufficiency, and effectiveness. If experience concludes it to be without purpose, irrelevant, outdated, or in some other way without profit, experience is wrong. Faith ought to stop us short every time we are tempted to skip through or over any portion of God's holy Word just because we are not immediately blessed. Before giving up on the passage, we should ask ourselves this question: Why, of all the possible things that God could have said, did He say this? By faith, we know why He said it—"that the man of God may be complete, thoroughly equipped for every good work" (2 Tim. 3:17). It remains for us to learn, understand, and apply what He said. The Scripture is the means by which God reveals, not conceals, truth.

Yet even here we must be realistic. To assume that we will understand everything in Scripture with equal ease is to reduce the Bible to a document that is less than ordinary and to set ourselves up for more frustration when we do not immediately get the point. The statement of the Westminster divines is a good and comforting reminder:

> All things in Scripture are not alike plain in themselves, nor alike clear unto all: yet those things which are necessary to be known, believed, and observed for salvation, are so clearly propounded and opened in some place of Scripture or other, that not only the learned but the unlearned, in a due use of the ordinary means, may attain unto a sufficient understanding of them. (Westminster Confession of Faith, 1.7)

God has made enough of His Word so crystal clear that only blind and blatant disbelief will not understand. He has made enough of His Word so deep that even the most faithful must depend on His enlightenment rather than their intellect. There is no book like the Bible—clear enough to speak to the layman, yet challenging enough to keep the scholar humble. Neither layman nor scholar should ever tire of this special revelation but should endeavor to increase the sphere of knowledge necessary to understand more and more. There is always more blessing to enjoy.

The key that unlocks the meaning and all the blessing of Scripture is the Lord Jesus Christ, the principal theme of the entire Bible. The overriding purpose of special revelation—which for us is the Scripture alone—is to guide men to a proper relationship with God. God's gracious salvation is the only way guilty sinners can experience that relationship, and God's gracious salvation is in and through His Son, the Lord Jesus Christ. The Lord Jesus Himself declared that He was "the way, the truth, and the life," the only way for anyone to come to God (John 14:6). It follows that if the purpose of Scripture is to guide people to the Lord and if the only way to the Lord is through the redemption of Jesus Christ, then the revelation of Christ should be the grand and predominant theme of Scripture. Indeed, it is. All revealed truth in one way or another relates to and is ultimately defined by the central truth of the Messiah, the Christ, the anointed. Obviously, the New Testament develops this saving theme. The Gospels, with narratives concerning His earthly ministry, introduce the performance of His saving work, the historic foundation of the gospel. Acts records the initial proclamation and dissemination of the message of His saving work. The Epistles explain and expound the nature of His person and work and the implications for personal and church life. The Revelation assures the consummation of all the glorious truths of His person and work. Understanding the message of the New Testament is impossible without reference to Christ.

Understanding the Old Testament is also impossible without reference to Christ and His gospel. He is the key that unlocks all the mysteries. This is not speculation; this is the teaching of the New Testament, both by direct statement and by example. When the resurrected Christ walked with the two disciples on the road to Emmaus, He expressed His concern that they were slow to believe what the prophets had written concerning His suffering and glory (Luke 24:25–26). He then started with Moses and continued through the Prophets, expounding what those Scriptures taught about Himself (Luke 24:27). Later in the company of all the disciples, He included the Psalms in that corpus of messianic revelation (Luke 24:44–45). His reference to Moses, the Prophets, and the Psalms was the Jewish designation for the entire Old Testament, similar to our referring to the New Testament as the gospel and Epistles. In other words, Christ said that the entirety of the Old Testament spoke about Him. The Pentateuch, the first five books with all their religious rituals, prepares the way for the Perfect Priest to stand between God and the people He represents as the perfect sacrifice for sins. The Historical Books draw attention to the Perfect King, who would come to rule His people and subdue His enemies. The Prophets anticipate the Perfect Prophet, who represents and reveals the only true and living God. The Poetical Books put it all together with the Christ as the great theme for worship and praise. What an authoritative clue for interpretation this is! It means that if we read any book of the Old Testament without reference to what it teaches concerning Christ, we are missing the key element in the book. If we do not see Christ, it is not because He is not there.

This brings us to the special issue of this series, the Gospel According to the Old Testament, and this book highlighting the gospel according to Hosea. The aim of the series is to show the pervasiveness of Christ in the Old Testament and to encourage all who read, teach, or preach from the Old Testament to do so with a view to Christ and His gospel. The book of Hosea, like every Old Testament book, lends itself to this approach. Much of Hosea's message parallels the points of the sermons preached by most of his prophetic and ministerial counterparts: God hates sin, God judges sin, God delivers from judgment upon repentance. Each of these points certainly has gospel implications. Yet, as is true regarding all of God's servants, there was something unique about Hosea, his ministry, and his message. His life and preaching exhibit a transparency that clearly points to Christ, but they also evidence a deep complexity that places his prophecy among the most difficult to understand in the Old Testament. But whether we look on or under the surface, Christ is the key to meaning. Discovering Hosea's inspired contribution to the progression of God's redemptive revelation is the goal of our study.

To say that Christ is the key to understanding Hosea is not to say that He is the only specific theme in the book, but it is to say that every other truth or command must find its ultimate reference in Him. To attempt to implement anything the Bible requires without reference to Jesus Christ is folly, whether it pertains to Old Testament or New Testament truth. The same principle applies to Hosea. It is beyond the scope of this book to treat exhaustively every verse in Hosea; this is not a commentary. Rather, this will be a theological overview of Hosea's message with a view to its gospel application. Searching for Christ in Hosea is not a vain game of hide and seek; finding Him is a sure thing. God's promise is that those who seek Him will find Him. So as we study Hosea, we want to be on Christ-alert.

I will develop the study in three parts. Part 1 concerns necessary issues of introduction. Introduction is that discipline of study that deals with such matters as authorship, date, historical background, purpose, and theme of writing. Although these may not be the most exciting or edifying elements of Bible study, they are essential facts that help to put a book in its context. Knowing both the historic and the canonical contexts of any book of the Bible is a significant aid and safeguard to proper interpretation. It is important to see where Hosea fits in the progress of both redemptive history and revelation. Part 2 develops the symbolic message of Hosea—his marriage to Gomer.

Unquestionably, the link between Hosea's personal life and his public ministry is unique and therefore critical for the understanding of the message. Understanding the theology of marriage as a biblical symbol and type of God's relationship to His people and specifically of Christ's relationship to His church is essential to grasping the significance of Hosea's experience. The significance of his tragic experience highlights the beauty of the ideal relationship that exists between Christ and His bride. Part 3 establishes the parallels between Hosea's life and the message he preached. If his marriage to Gomer was the symbolic message, his direct message concerns God's marriage to Israel. What Hosea did for Gomer, God did for Israel. What Gomer did to Hosea, Israel did to God. It was a relationship initiated by divine love, spurned by treacherous sin, and maintained by unfailing divine faithfulness. Although many of Hosea's statements are deep and difficult, his overall gospel message is very much on the surface. This particular part of the study will lend itself to the aim of the series to show the gospel in the Old Testament.

Please remember that in this study I am concerned with the big picture of Hosea, not the minute details. Our interest is in why and how the parts fit together to advance the revelation of the Christ and the gospel, rather than a technical exegesis to interpret all the specific parts. There are commentaries for that. So while I acknowledge that all the problems of interpretation may not be resolved, it is my prayer that throughout this study the Lord Jesus Christ will be evidently set forth and that the Holy Spirit will lead into truth by showing Christ and glorifying Him.

PART ONE

JUST THE FACTS

The Bible did not fall to earth from heaven complete and leather-bound. Different men—all of whom were inspired by the Holy Spirit—wrote the Old Testament over a period of about a thousand years. But each one lived in his own time and place; each one reflected and addressed the specific issues of his day. The truths of the Bible are universally and timelessly relevant, but they were first given to a specific people at a specific time to meet specific needs. The ultimate objective of our Bible study is to understand those universal and timeless truths and to apply them to our specific times and needs. An important part of Bible study is to learn what we can about the author, his times, and his particular circumstances. So here are just some facts about Hosea—the man and the book.

CHAPTER ONE

HOSEA: A MESSIANIC MAN

Hosea, the prophet, shared his name with other prominent characters in the Bible—some good, some not so good. Names are often significant in the Old Testament, certainly more so than they are in our culture. For us a name is a means of getting someone's attention or distinguishing and identifying one person from another. What a name means is sometimes a point of curiosity or a cute motto for a plaque or coffee cup, but hardly an element that conveys essential information about a person. My parents named me Michael ("who is like God?"), not because they were making a theological assertion but because for whatever reason they liked the name. My wife bought me one of those coffee cups with an inscription that supposedly defines *Michael*, but it says nothing about the Hebrew etymology of the name and instead has some flattering aphorism that I can only wish were true. The point is we use names without necessarily thinking about what the name means. In the Scripture, however, names often made a statement.

Names sometimes conveyed something about the nature, character, or behavior of the one so named. "You shall call His name JESUS: for He will save His people from their sins" (Matt. 1:21). That *Jesus* means "Jehovah saves" is certainly a significant statement given the purpose of the Savior's birth. Interestingly, the Greek name for Jesus corresponds to the Hebrew name *Joshua*, which is a lengthened form of *Hosea*, meaning "salvation." Joshua, the successor to Moses, sometimes went by the shorter name Hoshea (Num. 13:16; same as Hosea in Hebrew) and certainly his career of delivering the nation victoriously into the Promised Land corresponded to the name. But, on the other hand, Hoshea was also the name of Israel's last king, who ironically delivered the defeated nation into exile from the Promised Land (2 Kings 17:6). So what's in a name, after all?

Whether or not Beeri and his wife named their son *Hosea* either in hope or in anticipation of what he would do when he grew up is ultimately irrelevant. That Hosea's name means "salvation" is not a clue to the meaning, theme, or purpose of his prophecy, but it nonetheless is a fitting appellation to sum up his prophecies that so wonderfully declare God's sovereign grace in dealing with the undeserving. Salvation—that's a statement! Whether intentional or not, his name encapsulated his message.

Hosea's name says a lot, but it doesn't say it all. There is more to a man than his name—even when the names are as transparent as those of Old Testament characters. Much of Hosea's message relates to his personal life that became such a public one. But before considering the intimate details of that connection, we need to go over some basics about his office and place of employment or ministry that will help shape our understanding of the significance, sobriety, and authority of his message.

HIS PROFESSION

Ironically, notwithstanding the very public nature of Hosea's home life that provided the main points for his sermons, the Bible reveals very little about who Hosea was. Apart from identifying his father Beeri, the Scripture says nothing more about Hosea's lineage, unless the Beeri of Hosea 1:1 is to be identified with the Beerah of 1 Chronicles 5:6. If those two are the same, Hosea would be of the tribe of Reuben. But that is speculative and ultimately irrelevant apart from confirming his northern roots. The details of his lineage are immaterial because of his profession: Hosea was a prophet. Of the three anointed or messianic occupations—prophet, priest, and king—only the prophetic office was unrestricted regarding pedigree. Priests had to trace to Levi; kings (at least those of the southern kingdom) had to trace to Judah, and even more specifically to the family of David. So whereas priests and kings were born to be priests and kings, prophets became prophets only by the special call of God. Interestingly, whereas priests and kings could not cross over into the spheres of the other's operation, prophets could be priests, kings, or anything else. For the prophet, everything depended on God's call. Understanding something about the prophetic profession or office is prerequisite to understanding the significance of Hosea's ministry. Significantly, understanding something about the prophetic office enhances understanding about how Hosea contributes to the declaration of the gospel. The very fact that Hosea was a prophet points to the Lord Jesus Christ.

A Messianic Occupation

I've already referred to the prophetic office as a messianic occupation. The noun *messiah* is based on a verb meaning "to spread a liquid over."[1] The liquid most often used was olive oil, and the objects were both things and people. Most of the anointed objects had some function in the ceremonies of worship rituals. For instance, Exodus 29:36 instructs that the altar should be anointed after a sin offering. Exodus 40:9–11 includes, in addition to the altar, the laver and the entire tabernacle with all its vessels for the purpose of sanctifying the objects. Sanctifying refers simply to the separation of those objects from other things; the anointed objects were set apart for a distinct purpose and use. They were consecrated or dedicated to a particular function. The same meaning applies to the people anointed. The people anointed were usually in some leadership role, either civil or religious leadership: the most common were kings (1 Kings 1:34), priests (Ex. 28:41), and prophets (1 Kings 19:16). In each instance, the anointing was a symbolic gesture of setting the person apart for a special work. The commonly acknowledged association between the olive oil and the Holy Spirit is an important element in the ritual that adds to its significance.[2]

Although the Old Testament uses the noun *messiah* most frequently of kings (28 out of 39 occurrences), any person anointed could be accurately designated as a messiah. Kings, priests, prophets—all were messiahs. The noun form *messiah* in Hebrew conveys essentially the passive idea of the verb: a messiah is one who has been anointed. Being anointed identified the person as being qualified and consecrated for a special task. In other words, there was to be an active demonstration of the office to which the passive anointing pointed. An anointed king was to rule; an anointed priest was to minister; an anointed prophet was to preach. They were all "lesser" messiahs whose functions pointed to the Ideal Messiah who was to come and would fulfill perfectly every messianic operation. Three marks are common to every messianic function.

An Appointed Position. First, a messiah was a *divinely chosen* individual. This was true for kings (Deut. 17:15). It was true for priests (Deut. 18:5; Num. 17). It was true for prophets (Deut. 18:15, 18). Although not every prophet recounts the details or occasion of his call to the ministry, I would suggest that the detailed record of Jeremiah's call to the prophetic office is paradigmatic for every other true prophet (Jer. 1:4–10); therefore, it is instructive regarding Hosea.

The Lord's word to Jeremiah in Jeremiah 1:5 is particularly informative: "Before I formed you in the womb I knew you; [b]efore you were born I sanctified you; and I [appointed] you a prophet to the nations." Three verbs express the nature of the divine choice. The Lord said that He *knew* him. This is more than simple awareness or intellectual knowledge. It is, rather, an intimate, special, and selecting knowledge. This knowledge is part of the Old Testament's vocabulary of election. Humanly speaking, God knew Jeremiah before there was anything to know. The Lord then said that He *sanctified* him. Before he was born, God had set Jeremiah apart for the special purpose of being a prophet. His service was divinely determined before he knew what was happening. Finally, the Lord said that He *appointed* him to be a prophet. This verb has the normal meaning "to give," but also has the special sense of appointing or assigning to a specific task. God chose Jeremiah to be prophet; He called Jeremiah to be a prophet; and Jeremiah was a prophet. So it was for Hosea and, indeed, for every other true prophet.

What God determined in heaven happened on earth. There was no slip between the eternal purpose and the temporal fulfillment of God's intent. There never is. That's an important messianic lesson, particularly regarding the certainty of God's purpose in redemption. But it is, as well, an important lesson for everything in life, and for everyone's life. It was certainly true for Hosea. What Hosea preached and what he had to endure in connection with his ministry were the temporal manifestation of God's eternal plan. We may know nothing of the occasion and the details of Hosea's call, but the fact of the call is evident from its consequence. The Lord's beginning to speak by Hosea (Hos. 1:2) is irrefutable verification that he was

God's select spokesman, His prophet. Just as God raised Jeremiah to speak for Him in the final hours of the southern kingdom, so He raised Hosea before Him to preach to the northern kingdom on the eve of its destruction.

An Authoritative Position. Second, a messiah was an *accredited* individual. He had the authority to exercise his office. The prophet's authority rested in the fact that he was the representative of God before men, speaking the Lord's word to men. The Hebrew word translated "prophet" implies something of the inherent authority in the prophet's words. It is formed from a verb that most likely means simply "to speak." The word *prophet* evidences the same pattern as the word *messiah* in that it conveys the passive idea of the verb. A prophet, therefore, is one who has been spoken to and who in turn conveys that divine message to men. The only legitimate prophetic word—whether predicting the future, exposing sin, or inviting repentance—was "thus says the Lord God" (Ezek. 2:4).

Perhaps one of the clearest statements that the prophet was God's messenger with God's message is Haggai 1:12–13. Verse 12 actually equates obeying the voice of the Lord God with obeying the voice of Haggai the prophet. Verse 13 identifies Haggai as the "Lord's messenger" speaking "the Lord's message." Although miracles and fulfilled prophecies were visible means to validate the authenticity of the prophet (Deut. 13:1–3; 18:21–22), his ultimate accreditation was his faithfulness in proclaiming the word of the Lord.

When self-proclaimed prophets voiced their opinions, God forthrightly dismissed them; they had no authority (see Jer. 14:14). But regardless of whether the people received or rejected the prophet's word, if the chosen prophet spoke the word of the Lord, then one way or another there would be evidence that a prophet had been there (Ezek. 2:5). The sin, rebellion, and unbelief of the people would often rob a prophet of honor, but they could not nullify his authority. The authority of the prophet was in the Word. At the very beginning of his prophecy, even in the biography section, Hosea cites evidence of the Lord's speaking to him (see for examples 1:1, 2, 4, 6, 9; 3:1). Significantly, he begins the preaching section of his prophecy, "Hear the word of the LORD" (4:1).

An Energized Position. Third, a messiah was an *empowered* individual. When the Lord anointed one for some sphere of service, He did not abandon that individual to his own abilities or ingenuity. The Lord always supplied the power for that service, with the ultimate agent of power being the Holy Spirit. This empowering for service would have been the most vivid element in the anointing ceremony. As the olive oil was poured and smeared on the head of the appointed "messiah," so the Holy Spirit came upon him to enable him to perform the ministry for which he was being consecrated, as the passages below illustrate.

Although there is no direct statement of Hosea's empowerment or inspiration by the Holy Spirit, fulfilling his office responsibilities required it. What we read of this experience in the ministry of some prophets illustrates the common experience of all. Immediately after his call to the prophetic office, Ezekiel witnessed a mysterious and magnificent vision of God's absolute glory and fell on his face in worship and recognition of self-insufficiency. Then the Lord commanded him to stand, and the Spirit entered him and caused him to stand (Ezek. 1:28–2:2). Contrasting his ministry with that of false prophets, Micah testified, "But truly I am full of power by the Spirit of the Lord, and of justice and might, to declare to Jacob his transgression and to Israel his sin" (Mic. 3:8). The Lord assured Isaiah in connection with a profound prophecy of the Redeemer coming to Zion, "My Spirit who is upon you, and My words which I have put in your mouth, shall not depart from your mouth . . . " (Isa. 59:21). So the Spirit's empowering prophets enabled them to fulfill their duty of obeying God's commands, to preach with boldness regardless of opposition, and to do so with the confidence of the ultimate success of the word they preached.

Because he was a true prophet representing the one true and living God, Hosea shared these marks with every other of his messianic colleagues. The certainty of his divine call, his God-given authority, and his Spirit-enabled ministry added weight to what he preached and what he practiced. Hosea, like all his divinely called and inspired counterparts, was a preacher and reformer whose agenda was to motivate the people to repentance and to direct them to obedience to God's covenant demands. Israel, then, was to look, to hear, and to heed. We, now, are to do the same, since his message is the Word of God that abides forever.

A Messianic Anticipation

A picture is worth a thousand words—so they say. I'm not sure that we can make such a precise equation, but there is no question that pictures effectively communicate ideas and that illustrations can effectively aid our understanding. Just consider how many toys or appliances have been assembled by the owner's looking at the pictures rather than reading the instructions. Instructors often use visual aids to grasp or hold their students' attention as well as actually to impart the desired information. Sunday school teachers have for years used flannelgraph stories, object lessons, and wordless books with colored pages to teach youngsters about the gospel. Graphs, charts, and more sophisticated analogies aid even adults, with their greater attention spans and more advanced knowledge, to learn more easily.

From the beginning of His revelation, God has communicated in comprehensible ways. It is not surprising, therefore, that God, the most effective teacher ever, would communicate His truth with analogies, pictures, illustrations, and object lessons to clarify the profound and vitally important revelation He was graciously giving, not the least of which was the revelation of the Messiah. The Lord Jesus Himself, the Master Teacher, often pointed to something in the real world—whether a fig tree or a temple stone—to make a spiritual point. Similarly, the apostle John in the book of Revelation relies heavily on symbols to convey his message. So pictures are not just an Old Testament method of revelation.

When those pictures are also predictive, we call them types. It is beyond the scope of this study to review the nature and the hermeneutics of typology except to emphasize that typology is not an interpretation technique arbitrarily imposed on the Old Testament in an effort to rescue it for Christian relevance. Rather, it is a method of divine revelation. Let me put it simply in terms of "X" and "Y." If *X* is the picture and *Y* is the truth, God was saying to look at *X* in order to understand something about *Y*. Much of what we read in the Old Testament is God's using X's to teach ultimate truths about Y. The principal thing to remember is that X does not equal Y. So X is the type, the object lesson that foreshadows or predicts the actual, future realization of the pictured truth. Y is the antitype, the future realization to which the type points. The type represents and resembles the antitype. This does not mean that X loses its significance or usefulness in communicating the truth. We can still look at the picture and learn about the reality. The key point is that Christ is the ultimate reality: He is the Ideal behind—or perhaps I should say above—all the visible impressions.

These Old Testament picture prophecies, or types, fall into three categories: people, things, and events. For now our interest is the people. Certain people were types of Christ not because of their personalities or character traits, but by virtue of their office. All prophets, priests, and kings were lesser messiahs and types of the Ideal Messiah. All the features that mark them for their offices are perfectly and ideally true of the Lord Jesus Christ. He was chosen in the covenant of redemption to be the only redeemer of God's elect. He was accredited with heaven's approval and authority to perform all the duties of the anointed Mediator. He was empowered by the Holy Spirit for His work as the Savior. The Westminster Confession of Faith summarizes well the evidence of Scripture:

> It pleased God, in His eternal purpose, to choose and ordain the Lord Jesus, His only begotten Son, to be the Mediator between God and man; the Prophet, Priest, and King. . . . The Lord Jesus, in His human nature thus united to the divine, was sanctified and anointed with the Holy Spirit, above measure . . . to the end that . . . He might be thoroughly furnished to execute the office of a mediator and surety. Which office He took not unto Himself, but was thereunto called by His Father, who put all power and judgment into His hand, and gave Him commandment to execute the same. (8.1, 3)

A prophet, a priest, and a king are essential needs for the human race, whose sin necessarily separates its members from God and precludes them from approaching God on their own. Before the fall, Adam, the head of the human race, enjoyed a perfect communion and fellowship with God, his Creator. But with the fall came a tragic and drastic change in human nature and the loss of any relationship with the Lord. Iniquity separated mankind from God, and sin hid God's face (Isa. 59:2). When Adam fell, he and all his posterity lost the knowledge of God that must be renewed if there is to be salvation from sin (Col. 3:10). Humanity needed *a prophet* to reveal God. When Adam fell, he and all his descendants lost the righteousness and true holiness enjoyed at creation (Eph. 4:24). Mankind needed *a priest* to reconcile it to God. When Adam fell, he and all his seed became prey to the enemy of the soul who had power to hold them subject to bondage (Heb. 2:14–15). Mankind needed *a king* to reign, to subdue every enemy of the soul. What was needed, God in His wondrous and amazing grace provided in the person of His own dear Son, His and our Messiah. As the ultimate and ideal Messiah, the Lord Jesus Christ brought together in His single person all the common features shared by the lesser messiahs and all the specific duties and responsibilities of each of the three distinct offices. The Lord Jesus Christ did it all.

Our focus here is specifically on the prophetic office. The Lord Himself initiated this messianic anticipation with His promise to Moses that He would raise up "a Prophet" (Deut. 18:18), and statements in the New Testament testify to the expectant arrival of that ideal prophet (see, for instance, Matt. 21:11, 46; Luke 7:16; John 7:40). Every passing prophet increased the anticipation for *the* Prophet: When will He come? In one sense, every prophet shared the mission of John the Baptist, the greatest of the prophets before *the* Prophet, to prepare the way for His coming. As the fullness of time approached, the expectancy intensified. Remember that John was conducting such a remarkable ministry that some wondered and questioned if he was the promised Prophet (John 1:21). He set the record straight by identifying himself as the voice of one crying to prepare the way of the Lord; he made it clear that he was a pointer to Christ (John 1:23). That is the mission of every prophet, and by the very fact of his being a prophet he achieved that mission.

The Westminster Shorter Catechism succinctly defines how Christ carries out the prophetic office: "Christ executeth the office of a prophet, in revealing to us, by his word and Spirit, the will of God for our salvation" (question 24). Put simply, a prophet is God's representative to man. Who better than the very Son of God, Himself God, could represent God to man? Speaking of the Lord Jesus in prophetic terms, Hebrews declares that God spoke in various ways through the prophets but has now revealed His final word to man by His Son (Heb. 1:1–2). Although all the Old Testament prophets, including Hosea, were spokesmen for God and men of God, how imperfectly they represented God when compared to the Lord Jesus, who was "the brightness of His glory and the express image of His person" (Heb. 1:3). Similarly, Paul said of Christ that He is "the image of the invisible God" and that "in Him dwells all the fullness of the Godhead bodily" (Col. 1:15; 2:9). The bottom line, then, is this: Jesus Christ is the Ideal Prophet because Jesus Christ is God. The proof that Jesus of Nazareth is the Ideal Prophet was and is overwhelming. Christ's preaching, teaching, and working during His earthly mission constituted what we call His *immediate* or direct prophetic work. He consistently claimed the divine source of His message, predicted the future accurately, and performed the necessary signs and wonders to confirm His election, authority, and ability as *the* Prophet with the last and final Word from God. To Him, all the prophets bore witness.

Every lesser messiah was a type—a picture prophecy—of the ideal Messiah. It was said of Joshua and his attendants that they were "a wondrous sign" (Zech. 3:8). As priests, they represented and pointed to the coming Christ. The same can be said of Hosea, the prophet. As one of the lesser messiahs, Hosea contributed to God's revelation of the gospel by his status as a prophet as well as by the messages he preached. The Lord says to look at a prophet and to learn something about Christ. In his messianic role, he signaled the coming Christ. His presence among the people heralded that One who was certain to come. Hosea was one of God's installments on the prophetic line leading purposefully and unfailingly to the Ideal Messiah. Hosea was a contributor to messianic expectancy; therefore, we are to look at Hosea and learn of Christ. There is a sense in which every Christian is to be a sign of and to Christ. By our lives and words, we are to represent Christ and to point to Him. As a prophet, Hosea was a little messiah. As Christians, we are "little christs."

HIS PROPHECY

Called by God to be a prophet, Hosea was given a message to preach and a people to whom he would preach it. What he preached, both symbolically by his life and directly through his sermons, is the principal concern of the theological survey in Parts 2 and 3. My intention now is simply to identify his congregation, the overall scheme of his prophecy, and its place in the canon.

HIS PARISH

Hosea is unique among the writing prophets in regard to his nationality and parish. He was a citizen of the northern kingdom, and he directed his message principally to the northern kingdom. He was a northerner preaching to the north. In typical prophetic style, he introduced his prophecy by identifying the kings during whose administration he ministered (Hos. 1:1). His reference to Jeroboam, the king of Israel, hints at this northern heritage and concern. Interestingly, notwithstanding his northern connection, he lists all the kings of Judah from Uzziah to Hezekiah while ignoring the successors to Jeroboam whose reigns would have coincided with the Judah regents. Given the chaotic nature of the successions, marked by power struggles, political intrigue, assassinations, dynasty shifts, and brief tenures, it is of little wonder that Hosea disregarded naming the final kings of Israel. Jeroboam II had already put the nation on the slippery slope, and everything went quickly downhill after him. On the other hand, Hosea's specific inclusion of the Judean kings may say something of his theological, if not political, allegiance to the Davidic dynasty in view of what had to be his prophetic understanding of the Davidic covenant, which set the course for the coming of the Ideal King, his Savior. He anticipated His coming when he predicted the day in which Israel would return to the Lord their God, even David their king (Hos. 3:5). We'll get to that later.

Hosea was not the only prophet that God ever raised for a northern ministry. Like Hosea, Amos preached to Israel during the reign of Jeroboam II (Amos 1:1), but he was a missionary from the south. Jonah was from the north and also preached during the days of Jeroboam II (2 Kings 14:25), but his prophecy is biographical, recounting his reluctant mission to Nineveh. Elijah and Elisha, perhaps the most famous of the northern prophets, preached a century earlier, but were not counted as writing prophets.[3] Hosea's uniqueness, then, is the fact that he was a northerner who not only preached in the north but also wrote his message that was primarily directed to the northern kingdom. Yet as the inspired Word of God, borders do not restrict its authority and relevance.

One thing stands out in the light of the prophetic activity in the northern kingdom: in times of crisis, God sent a man with a word. At the inauguration of the kingdom, God sent a bold, yet naively disobedient, unnamed prophet to deliver a word against Jeroboam I when he set up what was to become the state religion of Israel (1 Kings 13). When Baal worship attained official status during the "co-regency" of Ahab and Jezebel, God raised up Elijah and then Elisha to affirm the one, true, and living God (1 Kings 17–2 Kings 13). At the beginning of the end when Jeroboam II ruled, God had His prophets—including Hosea—to sound the warning. Hosea's parish was ecumenical in the worst way: the state religion of Jeroboam I was entrenched and Baal worship lingered. Per the Lord's assurance to Elijah, it would be safe to assume that there was also a remnant according to grace (1 Kings 19:18).

The very fact that God raised up Hosea to minister to a people living in such a day of "religious mess" should give us hope. It doesn't require much spiritual insight to recognize the religious mess of our day. Religious pluralism plagues society, and true Christianity, which necessarily is exclusive, is at odds with the majority. Let it be our prayer that God would raise up ministers today with a prophetic boldness to declare His Word. In His grace, God has given His Word as the answer to any crisis.

HIS BOOK

God told every prophet what to say; He told some prophets what to write. Although there is some dispute even among conservatives regarding the dating of some of the writing prophets, this writing ministry, in all likelihood, extended from the ninth to the fifth centuries B.C. Sometime during his prophetic career, God inspired Hosea to write. What he wrote was immediately canonical—the inspired rule of faith and practice—but in the collection process became the first of the corpus commonly designated as the Minor Prophets. Needless to say, these prophets are not minor in terms of their significance, ability, or authority but only in terms of the length of their writing when compared to Isaiah, Jeremiah, and Ezekiel, the Major Prophets. The rationale for how the books in this unit of Scripture were arranged is not immediately evident. It is not strictly an issue of chronology or length, but it seems to be a combination of both. Hosea was not the earliest of the Minor Prophets, but his book is the longest among the earliest. Thus, it heads the collection. The principal issue is not *where* it is in the Bible but *that* it is in the Bible. Hosea's being inspired by the Holy Spirit to write (2 Peter 1:21) guaranteed the canonicity of his writing and assured its preservation. Hosea's book is a part of God's forever enduring Word.

The purpose of this theological analysis of Hosea's gospel message will preclude a sequential consideration of his prophecy, but it may help by way of overview to see a simple outline of his development. A most cursory reading of Hosea recognizes two principal sections: 1–3 and 4–14. The first division includes, though not exclusively, biographical details that establish the foundation for Hosea's using his personal life as a spiritual analogy. The second division records his sermons. The broad outline is obvious; the details are not—evident from the fact of the chapter division disparities between the Hebrew and the English Bibles. The problem is that there seem to be no "on the surface" objective markers to indicate the prophet's transitions, unless perhaps the hope messages signal the movement (Hos. 1:10–2:1; 2:14–23; 3:4–5; 6:1–3; 11:8–11; 14:1–8).[4] As well, the charges of no faithfulness, no lovingkindness, and no knowledge of God made at the beginning of the second division may hint to the main points of development (Hos. 4:1). The bottom line is that there is no consensus, and much work remains to be done regarding the structural analysis of the book. Nonetheless, here is a brief outline that maps the general flow of thought.

I. Hosea's Personal Life: The Symbolic Message 1–3
   a. His marriage and children 1
   b. The application to Israel 2
   c. His reunion with his wife 3

II. Hosea's Prophetic Discourses: The Direct Message 4–14
   a. Evidence of ignorance of God and statement of hope 4:1–6:3
   b. Evidence of disloyalty to God and statement of hope 6:4–11:11
   c. Evidence of faithlessness to God and statement of hope 11:12–14:9

Although we are left to ourselves to decipher Hosea's table of contents, the theme of his message is on the surface and clear. God remains faithful to His covenant regardless of the gross unfaithfulness of Israel: although spurned, His love is constant. This is the heart of the gospel according to Hosea.

FOR FURTHER REFLECTION

1. How do you continue to benefit from Christ's mediatorial work?
2. God used Hosea's life to communicate the gospel. How should your life communicate the gospel message to those around you?
3. Although today's ministers are not prophets by Old Testament definition, what can preachers today learn about their ministry from their Old Testament counterparts?

CHAPTER TWO

HOSEA: THE TIME OF HIS LIFE

Hosea was a real man living in a real world. His society, culture, and times affected him just as ours do us. Sometimes the way we read the Bible obscures the fact of this influence. This is particularly true regarding the Old Testament prophets. Too often, Christians read these books in isolation from the historical context in which they were written, even though a prophet may have directed attention to that context by naming the kings who reigned during his ministry. Those regal references should be enough to set the stage, but our knowledge of Hebrew history is sometimes deficient. And given the order of books in the English Bible, even a faithful and systematic reading of the Bible from cover to cover does not especially aid the memory. There is considerable distance between the Historical Books and the Prophets, and the beauty and blessing of the intervening poetry easily overshadow the facts of the past. Nevertheless, it remains an important step in the interpretation of a particular prophet to take the historical clues and factor them into his message. Hosea's opening reference to Uzziah, Jotham, Ahaz, Hezekiah, and Jeroboam may not seem to say much, but it actually speaks volumes about the urgent need for his message. This historical setting helps us to understand why God instructed Hosea to say what he said and to do what he did.

Foundational to understanding history properly is the recognition that all history is ultimately redemptive, converging on Christ. Time is God's servant, and it unwaveringly obeys His will. Time is the kingdom of God's providence in which He governs all things to His eternally designated end. Be careful not to entertain any vague or incorrect conceptions about divine providence. I asked a seminary student one time to define providence. After the predictable student silence, he fumbled the response, "It's kind of like fatalism." After I labeled him a pagan and facetiously threatened to bring out the matches reserved for those making such unorthodox statements, I emphasized the important difference between divine providence and the fatalistic notion that whatever will be will be. A belief in providence recognizes that God has decreed the end from the beginning as well as all the necessary in-between things that contribute to and ultimately accomplish the intended end. It operates according to the divine wisdom that knows the best possible way to achieve the best possible end. Nothing happens by chance; everything happens according to God's wisdom. I'm saying this to emphasize that the time and the circumstances of Hosea's ministry were providentially ordered as part of God's plan unfailingly heading to the first fullness of time when Christ would appear. Nothing in Hosea's life was accidental; Hosea's ministry served in the progression of God's redemptive purpose. Therefore, identifying the time of his life is important.

THE DATES OF HOSEA

History consists of more than dates, but dates are part of history. Dates help to keep things in perspective. Assigning dates to biblical books is a little complicated since our calendar reckoning differs from what was used in either Old Testament or New Testament times. But since our reckoning system is what we know and use, we customarily insert our own dates into the ancient time line. Plugging in our dates does not always yield precise results, but neither should it be regarded as guesswork. Scholars use two kinds of evidence for establishing these dates: relative chronologies and absolute chronologies. Relative chronologies simply put names and events in sequential order. Absolute chronologies require the insertion of an actual calendar date in the sequence. These actual dates are often calculated from some ancient documentation that mentions an astronomical event, such as an eclipse. Although I am clueless as to how to calculate and deduce when and where eclipses occurred and will occur again, others, happily, are not. So we rely on those calculations and conclusions. The fortunate thing is that we have plenty of evidence from the ancient world, both from the Old Testament and from the people of Old Testament times, to establish fairly accurate chronologies—at least for the monarchic period. I'm not going to go into all the evidence for assigning a date to Hosea, but I do want to emphasize that the date is not just arbitrarily being pulled from some hat.

The list of kings in Hosea 1:1 covers a span of just over a century—a period of time obviously longer than Hosea's ministry. Jeroboam II of Israel and Uzziah of Judah began their reigns within a year of each other, 793 B.C. and 792 B.C. respectively. Hezekiah's period in office ended in 686 B.C. Hosea lived and preached sometime within these parameters, but obviously not for the entire period. There are some clues, however, that can narrow the time framework further while keeping us within the temporal borders—if we read between the lines. This may get a bit tedious, but stay with me.

Hosea predicts the fall of Samaria, the northern kingdom (Hos. 1:3). Throughout his prophecy, this event looms in the future. Since Samaria fell to the Assyrians in 722 B.C., it would seem that Hosea's ministry ended before the fulfillment of what he predicted. Yet, he does mention Shalman, most likely Shalmaneser V (Hos. 10:14). According to 2 Kings 17:3–6, this Shalmaneser imprisoned Hoshea, Israel's last king, and initiated the three-year siege of Samaria that ultimately brought down the kingdom. Consequently, Hosea's ministry must have extended to 727 B.C. when Shalmaneser began to rule Assyria, but not quite to the end of his rule in 722 B.C. that coincided with Samaria's fall.

Fixing the point within those two dates for the end of Hosea's tenure rests on the reference to Hezekiah. The chronology of Hezekiah is riddled with problems, and solving the riddle is beyond our immediate concern. But here are the salient issues. The end of Hezekiah's reign in 686 B.C. is fairly certain, but that is far too late to include Hosea. According to 2 Kings 18:2, he reigned for twenty-nine years, marking 715 B.C. as his inauguration—seven years after the fall of Samaria. The math is easy enough. But that date still seems to be too late in comparison to the other evidence in Hosea, and the relative chronologies between Judah and Israel evince apparent inconsistencies. Here's where it gets fun. I'll try to be clear, but it does get confusing.

Second Kings records a relative chronology with points of reference between Hezekiah and Hoshea that are unexpected given the absolute dates assigned to their individual reigns. Hezekiah's first year was Hoshea's third (2 Kings 18:1); Hezekiah's fourth year was Hoshea's seventh (2 Kings 18:9); and Hezekiah's sixth year was Hoshea's ninth and last (2 Kings 18:10). Without contest, Hoshea's last year was 722 B.C., so on the surface it's not immediately clear how Hezekiah's sixth year (722 B.C. per 2 Kings 18:10) could have been seven years before his first (715 B.C. per his twenty-nine year reign). On the basis of this relative chronology between Hezekiah and Hoshea, Hezekiah's first year would be 728 B.C. rather than 715 B.C. This, happily, provides a date agreeable with Hosea's evidence, but it yields a reign of forty-two years rather than the twenty-nine stated in 2 Kings 18:2. And to complicate matters, 2 Kings 18:13 marks Hezekiah's fourteenth year as the date of Sennacherib's invasion of Judah in 701 B.C., taking us back to 715 B.C. as Hezekiah's first year. There appears to be a contradiction, but any contradiction in the Bible is always only apparent. I told you that this would be a bit puzzling.

However, let me briefly offer a possible explanation. Most likely, in accordance with common practice, Hezekiah served as a co-regent with his father Ahaz before assuming the sole rule of the nation. If this assumption is correct, his co-regency began in 728 B.C. and his sole reign began in 715 B.C. The relative chronology with Israel reckons his co-rule, whereas the reference to Sennacherib is based on his sole rule. It is only fitting, therefore, that Hosea would acknowledge Hezekiah as king. Factoring in Hezekiah's co-regency dates with the other evidence regarding Shalmaneser and Samaria's fall would put the end of Hosea's ministry somewhere about 725 B.C. It all fits.

The only thing left is to narrow down the beginning of his ministry. Although Jeroboam II and Uzziah assumed their throne about the same time, Uzziah outlived Jeroboam, ruling Judah for fifty-two years (2 Kings 15:2). Jeroboam ruled for only forty-one years (2 Kings 14:23–29), putting his death at 753 B.C. That means that since Hosea preached during the administration of Jeroboam II, he had to have begun by 753 B.C. at the latest.

Thanks for staying with me. It seems as though we've been around the proverbial barn, but all this suggests dates for Hosea's prophecy beginning prior to Jeroboam's death in 753 B.C. and ending around 725 B.C., after Hezekiah's ascension but before Samaria's fall. This, of course, refers to the tenure of his ministry, not how long it took to write the book.

THE WORLD OF HOSEA

Dating the book is one thing; understanding the significance of the date is another. Factoring in what we know about Hebrew history with the overall history of the ancient Near East marks Hosea's time as a climactic point on the timeline of Israel's history. I have emphasized that all history is redemptive, the stage for divine providence to accomplish its eternal purpose. God had His reasons for what was happening in Israel and His ways for achieving His aim. The Old Testament reveals the reasons for Israel's situation; the political history of the ancient Near East unfolds the method by which God accomplished His purpose. The next chapter will detail the theological "why's" of Hosea's world; here, I want to overview what his world was like but without digressing to a detailed development of either Hebrew or Assyrian history. A macroscopic view of the history of both will suffice.

Before summing up Hosea's world, I need to issue a caveat about the evidence. Both sacred and secular resources supply the data for what we know about this time period, and sometimes the records conflict. This ought not to be a surprise in light of the nature of history and historical accounts. The database for history is everything past, but not everything past constitutes especially significant history. Writing history requires not only knowledge of what has happened but also some criteria for selecting from that corpus of knowledge what is significant. The very nature of history hampers historians because of their limited knowledge of the past, and it also breeds justifiable suspicion about every historical account because of the biased perspective of the recorder. In one way or another, every new generation of historians depends for knowledge in part on earlier records, which themselves suffer from the recorder's ignorance of all the facts and necessarily reflect some bias. The ancient chroniclers were usually employed by the royal court, and consequently they skewed facts in favor of the throne. It was their job to justify or glorify official policies and ventures and to create a legacy for the king. Today, we call them "spin doctors." Governments have always used them. Just because something is written in stone, it doesn't make it so.

Here's the point. If writing a truly important and accurate history requires knowing everything about the past, as well as the ability to identify the salient parts from that body of knowledge, Scripture is the only truly significant history that exists. Only God is omniscient; only God is infinitely wise. Therefore, only God, the ultimate author of Scripture who knows everything, has the skill to select from what He knows to record a history that is both infallibly accurate and eminently significant. So at whatever point secular history disagrees with sacred history, we know that the secular historian was either mistaken about the facts or misleading in how he presented the facts. We can be certain of two things as we read the Bible: it is true, and it is important. Nothing ever written is more true, and nothing ever written is more important. This gives confidence as we use the Bible as our history text and raises caution as we use other sources. We believe that whatever the Bible says is true. What the other sources say may well be true, but we can't be as certain. So with this simple philosophy of history in mind and with my promise not to write a detailed account of Hebrew and Assyrian history, we're ready for the relevant facts of Hosea's world—at home and abroad.

His World at Home

The Old Testament supplies the points of interest. Israel had a checkered history from its inception, alternating between bad and worse. Tragically, the northern kingdom never had a good king. It had powerful and prosperous kings but never a good one. That assessment alone testifies to how differently the omniscient Historian evaluates significance. Military exploits, economic affluence, and building projects are usually the stuff of royal chronicles. The inspired histories typically glossed over these accomplishments and zeroed in on the king's moral character and his spiritual influence on the nation. For Judah, the standard was how well the king did in comparison to David; for Israel, it was how bad he was in comparison to Jeroboam I, who from the beginning taught Israel to sin.

As we've observed from Hosea's calendar of events, Hosea began his career toward the end of the administration of Jeroboam II. Although the Scripture refers to him simply as Jeroboam, we number him "II" to distinguish him from Jeroboam, the first king of the northern kingdom, whom we number "I." But the two were not related, which itself says something about the state of Israel. Whereas Judah's dynastic kings ascended to David's throne as evidence of God's covenant faithfulness (2 Sam. 7:12–16) and His unrelenting determination to set David's greater Son—His Son—on that throne (Ps. 2:6), Israel's kings could hardly get a dynasty going.[1] Israel was a kingdom marked by royal instability and insecurity.

Jeroboam II, the third in the line of Jehu, was the next-to-last king of Israel's fourth and longest dynasty (eighty-nine years). Were it not for the fact that God had promised Jehu a dynasty extending to four generations (2 Kings 10:30; 15:12), Jeroboam might as well have been the last. For all practical purposes, he was. His son Zechariah lasted only for six months before his assassination by Shallum, who in turn reigned for only a month before Menahem killed him (2 Kings 15:8–12). The early days of Hosea's ministry were marked by political intrigue and chaos—little wonder he didn't bother naming the kings after Jeroboam.

Notwithstanding all the political maneuvering and murdering, everyday life was pretty good, at least at the beginning of Hosea's prophetic career. Jeroboam II enjoyed significant military success, regaining territories to the north, south, and east that almost matched the borders of the glory days of David and Solomon in those regions (2 Kings 14:25, 28). His administration also fostered an economic prosperity that set a standard of living affecting all of society in one way or another. Luxury led to a materialism that translated into class divisions and struggles, with the rich becoming richer and the poor becoming poorer. Amos, the southern missionary to the north during the days of Jeroboam, is often characterized as the prophet against social injustice because of his pointed accusations of societal abuses. The extreme wealth among the people is manifested, for instance, in his references to seasonal vacation homes and residences filled with ivory (Amos 3:15). He attests to their selfish materialism in his condemnation of the wives of Samaria—whom he calls cows—who pressure their husbands to maintain their style of living even if it means extorting and taking advantage of others to do it (Amos 4:1). Hosea states the fact unequivocally when he quotes Ephraim—another name for Israel—as saying, "I'm rich" (Hos. 12:8). In many ways, life was good—at least for some.

Affluence, however, is seldom friendly to the gospel. It tends to breed carnal security and a self-confidence that cause the comfortable either to see no need for God or to interpret the ease of life as a token of God's favor. The same Ephraim that declared its wealth also professed its innocence by claiming it was free from iniquity (Hos. 12:8). So, for a prophet to announce God's displeasure and to threaten impending doom seemed to be incongruous with reality. Convincing a sinner of his sin is always prerequisite to pointing him to the gospel solution to his sin. Hosea, obviously conscious of that logic in evangelism, focused much of his message on exposing the sin of the people. He was dealing with a people whose spiritual callousness, hardened by material riches, desensitized them to spiritual matters. The good life, thanks to Jeroboam, made Hosea's job hard.

The good life provided by Jeroboam's leadership did not last; peace and prosperity gave way to foreign domination and economic deprivation. Repentance and spiritual renewal, however, did not ensue. It's not the environment, after all, that determines character or spiritual consciousness.

The fatal connection between Israel's foreign and domestic policies surfaced during the reign of Menahem (2 Kings 15:14–22). His predecessors, Zechariah (six months) and Shallum (one month), did not rule long enough to establish or enforce any kind of policy. My guess is that the conspiracies and violence that marked the transitions in power served only to create anxiety and uncertainty among the people. Well within a year of Jeroboam's long and stable reign (forty-one years), Israel saw three kings on the throne. They had to be wondering what was happening; it appeared their comfortable world was falling apart. Menahem brutally terrorized those who did not submit, to the extreme of savagely murdering pregnant women (2 Kings 15:16). He answered the Assyrian threat by paying Assyria tribute money, a foreign policy that he subsidized by imposing outrageous taxes on the wealthy (2 Kings 15:19–20). It bought a bit of peace with the Assyrians, but the cost was immense.

Not surprisingly, Menahem's dynasty was short-lived. His son, Pekahiah, ruled for only two years before Pekah assassinated him in what appears to have been a military coup (2 Kings 15:23–31). There is some evidence that Pekah had set up a rival government in the Transjordan during the administration of Menahem,[2] and perhaps the heavy taxation necessary to support the pacifistic policy with Assyria fostered the boldness to take military action. It seems that the concerns over the domestic economy always trumped the issues of foreign policy. Pekah's more aggressive military policy, evidenced in part by his ill-conceived alliance with Syria against Judah (2 Kings 16:5–7), led to an Assyrian invasion into Israel and the deportation of many of its inhabitants (2 Kings 15:29). And finally, there was Hoshea, Israel's last king. He ascended to the throne according to what had become typical procedure: conspiracy and assassination (2 Kings 15:30). Thanks to Pekah's policy, much of the land had already been lost to Assyria, so to preserve what little was left, Hoshea reverted to Menahem's policy of paying tribute money to buy a peace (2 Kings 17:3). For some reason, either depletion of resources, assistance from Egypt, or an increasing anti-Assyrian sentiment, Hoshea stopped payments and thus led his nation to its end (2 Kings 17:4–6). He was imprisoned, Samaria was besieged, and the people of Israel were exiled from home (2 Kings 17:5–6).

His World Abroad

Even a cursory survey of the world scene boldfaces the Lord's absolute sovereignty over all the affairs of the world to accomplish His purpose. Although the then-current events had military and political explanations that would have engaged the news media of the day, they confirm over and again the truth of Proverbs 21:1—"The king's heart is in the hand of the LORD, like the rivers of water; He turns it wherever He wishes."

Because God is totally sovereign, He can choose to work either with or without external means to accomplish His will. The Lord's behind-the-scene manipulation of nations was His primary method of executing the consequences of His will regarding Israel. This means of accomplishing His will showed itself most obviously when the time came for Israel to be expelled from the land because of their unbelief. Hosea warned the nation that their rampant idolatry disqualified them from the land and that judgment loomed. Hearing the threat, however, did not cause them to pack their bags and leave their homes on their own. As the biblical record highlighted, they did everything they could to maintain their homes, whether by mollification or through bravado. So the Lord used the Assyrians as His instrument to effect the expulsion. Isaiah, with prophetic insight, identified the Assyrians as the rod of God's anger (Isa. 10:5).

From a natural historic perspective, it is not surprising that the Assyrians were able to conquer Israel. By the eighth century B.C., Assyria, militarily and politically, had become the most powerful nation in the world of the Near East with their control extending throughout Mesopotamia all the way to Egypt. They ruled an empire. Secular accounts from the period[3] detail a military genius and cruelty that stood unmatched. Certainly, neither Israel nor Judah possessed military machinery sufficient to resist Assyrian advances. So from a natural perspective Israel's defeat at their hands is not surprising. From that same natural perspective what is surprising is that Assyria did not defeat Judah the same way. More was going on than the eye could see.

A detailed account of Assyrian history would be interesting but beyond the scope of what is relevant to our concern about Hosea's world. But Assyria was a part of Hosea's world, and the threat of Assyrian domination was a specific point in his preaching (Hos. 11:5). Understanding something about Assyrian strategy and policy gives a bit of insight into how God used this pagan power to accomplish His purpose.

As the borders of Assyria expanded to empire proportions, the Assyrian kings developed ingenious ways to consolidate and control their territorial interests. Both biblical and secular records illustrate the varied tactics, which seem to have been determined by the level of "trouble" being caused by the tributary. First, those pro-Assyrian nations willing to pledge allegiance to Assyria and pay tribute money to buy protection and maintain peace continued to enjoy a degree of national independence and identity, but at significant expense. This peace-at-any-cost was Menahem's course of action and Hoshea's at the beginning of his reign. Interestingly, Ahaz of Judah volunteered for this arrangement when he felt threatened by the Israeli-Syrian coalition, doing so against the advice of Isaiah (Isa. 7; 2 Kings 16:5–9). Second, those nations who rebelled and withheld the tribute payments became subject to invasion, which resulted in the loss of territory to Assyria's direct control. As part of this territorial incorporation, the Assyrian authorities deported many of the natives to other provinces. This is what happened during the reign of Pekah and would have happened during Hezekiah's reign had not God interrupted the normal course of events (2 Kings 19:35–36). Third, those nations whose rebellion persisted met Assyria's full fury: they were destroyed, and the population was even more thoroughly dispersed. This happened to Samaria after Hoshea stopped payment again and solicited support from Egypt. Assyria had had enough.

Most striking was the Assyrian policy of deportation used to control the conquered lands and people. It was an ingenious way both to demoralize a people and to reduce the threat of rebellion. An expatriated people would have little incentive to revolt in a land which was not their native soil. What is even more notable is the fact that in the history of warfare, this seems to be the first time such a tactic was employed. In the providence of God at the very moment when His patience with idolatrous Israel had expired and the time of their expulsion had arrived, there was a mechanism in place to accomplish His purpose. Let me pose this question: Where did the Assyrian commanders get the idea of deportation? Remember that Proverbs 21:1 says the king's heart is in God's hands.

Isaiah had it right when he identified Assyria as the rod of God's anger (Isa. 10:5). That Assyria was not successful against Judah underscores the truth that it was merely an instrument in God's hand. Militarily, Sennacherib should have had no difficulty carrying out his threats against Hezekiah, whose withholding tribute payments qualified Judah for the next stage of Assyrian reprisals—incorporation and deportation. But it was not yet time for God to execute His judgment on Judah, so Judah was preserved. God's direct intervention showed that He was the One in control. Without any human means, God caused the mighty army of Sennacherib to retreat in confusion after slaying 185,000 soldiers in the darkness of a single night (Isa. 37:36).

Although the Assyrians were ignorant of their manipulation by God and their role as the agents of providence, they were nonetheless subjects of God's kingdom. God certainly held them accountable for their transgressions against His law and dealt with them according to their works. Hosea lived in a world that was in God's hand, and he witnessed the absolute sovereignty of God using the events and circumstances of life to accomplish the very message he was preaching. In hindsight, it does not require much spiritual acumen to recognize God's amazing control over the nations of the Old Testament world. So now let me pose this question: At what point in the history of the world did God stop controlling the nations of the world?

In our hearts we know the biblically correct answer to this question. In our heart of hearts we know that God controls governments and the course of human events as much today as ever. Yet so often we live as though God at some point in history abdicated His throne in exchange for a bleacher seat. Too many Christians live as though God is pacing back and forth in heaven, wondering and worrying about what He will or can do if this or that happens on earth. At the very least, that is not a biblical view of God. If Hosea's world was in God's hand, so is ours.

The history of Hosea's world delineates the fulfillment of his prophecy that the Lord would first bring the demise of Jehu's dynasty and then the end of the whole kingdom of Israel (Hos. 1:4), and that He would do so at the hand of the Assyrians (Hos. 11:5). Hosea lived and ministered during most of that history and, therefore, preached to a nation on the brink of disaster. There was a sense of urgency to his message, but the nation was oblivious: Israel constituted a tough congregation. What Israel experienced in the swirling demise of their national sovereignty and standard of living consistently affirmed the veracity and authority of Hosea's message. Hosea was a true prophet: the evidence was irrefutable (Deut. 18:21–22). Would that they had been wise and understood (Hos. 14:9)!

Yet ironically and graciously, the tragic consequences of Israel's ignorant and foolish rejection of Hosea's message anticipated the grace of the gospel. Ironically, the territory of Israel that first experienced God's judgment (all the land of Naphtali, 2 Kings 15:29) was by God's grace the first region of Israel that would witness the ministry of Christ (Matt. 4:12–16). The darkness of Hosea's day would give way to the light of Christ. The time of darkness was a providentially ordered step toward the fullness of time in which the Light would shine. God's purposes and plans always come together.

FOR FURTHER REFLECTION

1. Review the major developments of God's redemptive plan.
2. Generally, how do we establish dates for Old Testament history?

3. What should be your attitude when the "facts" of secular history disagree with the "facts" of biblical history?
4. Why did the southern kingdom maintain a single dynasty of kings when the northern kingdom did not?
5. Why does prosperity sometimes conflict with the gospel?
6. Think about the ways in history that God manipulated pagan governments to accomplish His purpose. What are the implications for current events?
7. What is the irony of Christ's beginning His public ministry in Galilee?

CHAPTER THREE

HOSEA: HIS CREED

Current creedal or denominational labels cannot plausibly define Hosea's confession of faith or worldview since he lived so long before they assumed their current significance. But his focus on the covenant and his intent to reform appear in boldface in his prophecy, revealing both his theological basis and his agenda. Hosea, in the tradition of all his prophetic colleagues, was a reformer. Contrary to the hackneyed notions of the old rationalistic theologians, the prophets were not innovators introducing the next stage in the evolution of religion but reformers imploring the people to return to the old-time religion. Jeremiah's exhortation sums up the prophetic mission nicely: "ask for the old paths, where the good way is" (Jer. 6:16).

One's creed provides the framework for interpreting Scripture and viewing the world. A reformed and covenant creed generates a worldview markedly different from what a dispensational creed would; a Calvinist sees things differently from an Arminian. That is just the fact of the matter, and it is not uniquely limited to the systems of theology that compartmentalize the church today. The prophets—the Old Testament reformers—likewise interpreted their world from the perspective of a definite theological framework and foundation. For the prophets, including Hosea, Moses charted the course for faith; he laid the foundation for Old Testament reformation theology. Ultimately, there is little hope of understanding the prophets apart from understanding Moses. Specifically, there is little hope of understanding the prophets apart from understanding Deuteronomy, where Moses brings together the implications of covenant theology. Deuteronomy is both the cornerstone of the Pentateuch and the foundation for everything that follows.

For instance, one of the great themes in Deuteronomy concerns God's promise of the land. God first promised the land as an integral element in the covenant He made with Abraham and his seed (Gen. 12:7; 15:18; 17:8). That promise was unilateral and unconditional. Although the promise concerned real geographical territory whose borders can be found on a map, God infused the land with important spiritual and theological lessons. There was more to the land than dirt. Simply stated, throughout the Old Testament God used the land as an object lesson to represent the fullness of spiritual blessing. Rest in the land was associated with the experience and enjoyment of God's presence. So notwithstanding the ultimately unconditional aspect of the promise, individual participation in the promise was conditioned by faith. Thus, according to Hebrews 3:19, the wilderness generation did not enter the land "because of unbelief" (see also the argument of Psalm 95:8–11). This is where the theology of Deuteronomy applies. Not only did entrance into the land require faith; so did remaining in the land. Moses expressed clearly the terms of the land contract. First, if they kept the commandments and walked in the ways of the Lord, the Lord would bless them richly in the land (see Deut. 28:1–2, 8–13). Second, if they violated the commandments, particularly by going after other gods, the Lord would curse them (Deut. 28:14–15), primarily by plucking them out of the land and scattering them among the nations (Deut. 28:63–64).

Third, if they returned to the Lord, the Lord would exercise compassion and graciously gather them from wherever they were scattered and bring them back to the land (Deut. 30:2–3).

The checkered history of Israel mirrors each of these contractual points. Although their faith was not unwavering nor their obedience perfect, several high-water marks in Israel's spiritual development brought them victoriously into the land and enabled them to enjoy the promised prosperity and blessing. Sadly, it was not long before they tragically disobeyed and faithlessly pursued other gods. In keeping with His word, God expelled the people from the land, first the northern kingdom of Israel and then the southern kingdom of Judah. In one way or another all the prophets echoed Moses and warned of the impending judgment. It's almost as though the prophets instructed their congregations to open their Bibles to Deuteronomy and then expounded to them the Scripture.

Hosea is the topic of this study, so a detailed examination of Mosaic theology is not in order. Yet, since Hosea evidently took his "text" from Deuteronomy, a synopsis of the Mosaic themes that climaxed in this book will aid us in identifying Hosea's creed that governed his assessment of Israel's spiritual condition and that underlay the content of his own inspired message. At the core of Mosaic theology, and consequently at the core of Hosea's, is the covenant. At the core of the covenant is the gospel, the revelation of Jesus Christ. Significantly, then, the Lord's indicting the nation for transgressing His covenant (Hos. 8:1) is tantamount to His accusing them of rejecting the gospel. The covenant is serious business. Prerequisite, therefore, to comprehending the christological and gospel message of Hosea is understanding something of the essence of Old Testament covenant theology and its implications according to Moses.

THE ESSENCE OF COVENANT THEOLOGY

Here's the conclusion upfront: Christ is both the topic of covenant themes and the very heart of the covenant itself. It is the covenant promise of Christ that unifies the Old Testament and links it to the New Testament. Indeed, at the core of every covenant institution—whether with Adam, Noah, Abraham, Moses, or David—was the "better covenant," the Lord Jesus Christ Himself. Some attention to the definition and development of the covenant will prepare us for the ultimate objective of seeing the gospel in Hosea. I need to emphasize that understanding the gospel focus of the covenant is essential to understanding Hosea. He did not always reiterate the details of the covenant, but its significance was always in view. We must keep it in mind to get his point.

Definition of Covenant

Although we rarely use the word *covenant* in modern English apart from legal contracts and marriage ceremonies, it was a well-known concept in the Old Testament world and thus a most fitting vehicle by which God revealed Himself and His gracious promises to man. The word *covenant* (*berith*) occurs about three hundred times in the Old Testament. Opinions concerning the etymology of *berith* range from root words meaning "to fetter," "to eat bread with," or "to decide." This sort of speculation can be interesting, but it can prove distracting in the absence of any definite proof. When a word occurs as frequently in the Old Testament as *berith*, my opinion is that etymology is irrelevant and that the contexts of word usage better provide clues for definition. In view of all the Old Testament evidence, I would define *covenant* as a "mutually binding agreement between two parties." This agreement obligated the parties to certain duties and guaranteed certain issues.

Many of the covenant contexts recorded in the Old Testament were between parties of more or less equal standing. Because the parties were equal, the terms of agreement were often negotiable yet mutually binding once the deal had been struck. These are called parity or dipleuric contracts. Other covenants between superiors and inferiors are called suzerainty or monopleuric covenants. A suzerain is a sovereign, a king. These covenants were both non-negotiable and mutually binding. The sovereign had the right to set the terms to which the subjects submitted. In both the parity and the suzerainty covenants, all the parties assumed certain obligated duties that were guaranteed by a pledge of allegiance or oath. Obviously, in the covenant that God makes with men, He is the superior with the divine right to set all the terms and the divine power to fulfill His pledge.

Observing some of the attendant actions and events that occurred in conjunction with covenant ratifications also helps to define the concept. What happened in the human covenants prefigures what happened in the divine covenant and pales in comparison. First, an oath often accompanied the establishing of the covenant. Taking an oath, or swearing, was a pledge of allegiance to the terms of the covenant agreement and the declared promise to fulfill those terms (Gen. 26:28). The oath was the guarantee.

Second, a sacrifice was often an integral part of making a covenant (Gen. 31:54). Interestingly, the common designation for making a covenant was "to cut a covenant." The idiom was used even when no actual sacrifice occurred, but the act of sacrifice may clarify the expression. Jeremiah 34:18 is a key text that may provide some explanation. The Lord declared judgment on those who broke the terms of His covenant by not performing "the words of the covenant which they made before Me, when they cut the calf in two and passed between the parts of it." Theories abound concerning the significance of this act. I can only give my opinion. I think perhaps this part of the ceremony was to convey the reconciliation between the parties and in effect to declare what by covenant they now shared. The two halves most likely represented the two parties of the covenant, and the passing through the parts symbolically represented the binding of the parties into a single unit. Each had his part; each had his duty to fulfill in maintaining the agreement. It was a mutually binding contract.

Third, a fellowship meal was a common component of making a covenant (Gen. 26:30; 31:54; 2 Sam. 3:20). This is particularly significant because eating together signaled an affirmation of friendship and peace. Though speaking of betrayal, Psalm 41:9 clearly suggests this import of the common meal in referring to "my own familiar friend . . . [w]ho ate my bread." The fellowship meal indicated the reconciliation of the parties. Whatever it was that had alienated them was resolved, and they could sit together in peace.

Fourth, salt was sometimes associated with a covenant (see Num. 18:19; 2 Chron. 13:5). The symbolic significance of the salt was more likely in its use as a preservative than in its savory quality. The salt of the covenant asserted the continuing and perpetual aspect of the agreement. A covenant was not to be broken; it was a binding agreement.

All the salient features that define and identify covenants reach the ideal in God's gracious covenant. The major difference between the human-to-human agreements and the God-to-man covenant is that God could and would keep His end of the agreement. Men often reneged on the terms of their contracts, and sovereigns often made promises they were incapable of keeping. But God was—and is—unfailingly faithful.

Consider these covenant treaty features as they relate specifically to God's covenant of grace and see why I say the merely human covenants pale in comparison and why the covenant defines the core of Hosea's gospel.

1) As covenants were confirmed with oaths, so God confirmed His covenant promise of Christ with an oath. The prophet Micah ended his message with the assurance that God would perform the truth to Jacob and His covenant loyalty to Abraham, which He had sworn to the patriarchs from the beginning (Mic. 7:20). When reaffirming the covenant with Abraham, God swore by Himself (Gen. 22:16). The New Testament commentary explains that He did so because He could swear by nothing greater and because the oath was the direct means to give assurance of the unchangeableness of His purpose (Heb. 6:13, 17). Significantly, Hebrews immediately identifies the irrevocable promise as referring to the Lord Jesus Christ, the sure and steadfast anchor of the soul (Heb. 6:19). God, therefore, guaranteed with a pledge of infinite worth the certain coming and successful mission of Christ to fulfill every term and promise set down by covenant.

2) As covenants were ratified by sacrifice, so God ratified His gracious covenant by the sacrifice of His dear Son. Hebrews again gives us the inspired commentary that Christ as the mediator of the new covenant died to redeem sinners, even sinners under the old covenant (Old Testament believers), so that "those who are called may receive the promise of the eternal inheritance" (Heb. 9:15). It is not without significance that Jesus Himself in instituting the Lord's Supper referred to the cup as the new covenant in His blood (1 Cor. 11:25). Similarly, as the Old Testament covenant sacrifices pictured the reconciliation of the parties, so Christ "made peace through the blood of His cross" to reconcile all things to Himself, especially those alienated from God and enemies of Him (Col. 1:20–21).

3) As covenants were affirmed with communal fellowship meals, so God now receives to a place of peace and pardon those who have accepted Christ. Being justified by faith in Christ, we have peace with God and access by faith into grace (Rom. 5:1–2). Although there is perhaps

not a direct line of connection, I would like to suggest a link between this fellowship meal and what we experience at the Lord's Table. That we so often refer to this sacrament as "Communion" testifies to the enjoyment of peace and the experience of divine presence we know in union with Christ, the covenant promise.

4) As the salt of the covenant pictured the certain perpetuity of the covenant, so God has made Christ the surety, or guarantee, of the better covenant (Heb. 7:22). There is not the slightest possibility that any part of God's covenant promise regarding Christ can fail, because "all the promises of God in Him are Yes" (2 Cor. 1:20). By covenant, God has graciously and sovereignly entered into a binding agreement that He will save any and all who come to Him through the Lord Jesus Christ (see John 6:37). By covenant, He has obligated Himself to keep the promise. Christ is the guarantee of salvation.

I pray that this covenant concept will sink into our souls. It truly boggles the mind that the God who owes nothing to anyone obligates Himself to fulfill all the terms of the covenant and make good on every promise. The gospel of Christ is no "maybe" gospel; it must work or God is not God. As we consider the gospel according to Hosea, we must keep in mind this full definition of the covenant and not pass over its references or allusions lightly (remembering that the concept is more extensive than occurrences of the term *berith*). It is a theologically charged concept, and its prominence in Hosea is a key component of this gospel message.[1]

Development of Covenant

In order to justify my contention that Hosea's covenant theology was christological, I want to trace briefly the progressive development of covenant revelation that constituted the database of truth the prophet would have been aware of and that is, therefore, an essential component in interpreting his message. Bear with me in this survey; it is most relevant to our topic. And as a bonus, its relevance extends beyond Hosea to the whole of Scripture. Let me give a personal testimony. When the realization finally hit me in my hermeneutic journeys that Christ is the unifying theme of all the covenants, it was like the proverbial lightbulb going on in my head. This is a simple and profound thought, and why it took so long for me to recognize it speaks to my dullness. But to recognize in all the covenant institutions, with their particular elements and attendant circumstances, this single, constant, unchanging, unifying message has helped me immensely to discover God's purpose and irresistible, unfrustratable plan in providing the one and only Redeemer to save sinners. It is the covenant promise that unlocks the message of the Bible, unifies the Old Testament, and links it to the New Testament. I want us to understand what Hosea certainly did.

Although there is a single covenant of grace, God revealed the covenant at various stages of Old Testament history. Beginning in the garden of Eden and ending with the promised new covenant, God disclosed to man more and more about His plan and purpose for His people in Christ. The Edenic (Gen. 3), Noahic (Gen. 6–9), Abrahamic (Gen. 12–17), Mosaic (Ex. 19), Davidic (2 Sam. 7), and new (Jer. 31) covenants are not different covenants; they are the same covenant that God renewed and enlarged, each time revealing more and more of the essential details. Every promise of salvation made in these covenant installments focused on and culminated in Christ, but not every promise highlighted every aspect of christological truth. Each new institution renewed earlier promises and advanced knowledge about God's promise to reverse the curse.

Let me digress to define what I mean by progressive revelation. Because the nature of redemptive truth is complex, God progressively revealed truth in ways that man could understand. I have already suggested that the covenant theme was something man was familiar with and understood; it was an appropriate vehicle to communicate truth. Understanding complex ideas requires a comprehension of fundamental or elementary ideas. For instance, a grasp of the basic rules of mathematics and physics is essential to understanding quantum theory. Attempting to teach quantum theory to first graders would be disastrous, even if some in the class might eventually become brilliant physicists. Furthermore, full comprehension of the complexities of quantum theory does not imply a rejection of the basic rules of mathematics or physics. Advanced knowledge does not contradict or invalidate elementary knowledge; it builds upon it. I teach Hebrew classes ranging from elementary to advanced courses. I do not teach the beginning students what I teach the advanced, but everything I teach the advanced students rests on the foundation of what I teach the beginners. If I were to require my beginning students to know and do what I expect of my advanced students, I would most likely never again have advanced students. The casualty rate would be so high that none would be left to advance. So I go slowly (at least from my perspective), establishing foundations on which to build more understanding. This principle applies to all education.

And this, simply, is the nature of God's progressive revelation of redemptive truth. He gives first the foundation and continues to build, increasing the capacity to understand. Progressive revelation does not change the essence of truth; it expands, clarifies, and details the truth. Progressive revelation is never from wrong to right. It is from general to specific, from macroscopic view to microscopic view, from overview to thorough view. The foundational revelation has few components and broad definition; the advancing revelation adds more and more specifying, identifying, and defining components. The closer the promise gets, the clearer the details about the promise become. By Hosea's time, God had revealed much about the "Curse-Reverser" regarding both identity and work, and much of the revelation was in terms of the covenant. I offer this synopsis of the covenant development.[2]

Immediately after Adam and Eve sinned, God promised that the Seed of the woman would destroy the serpent. The first sinners received the direct, quite general, but most encouraging promise that a Savior for humanity would arise from the human race. Humanity had just been cursed by sin, and one coming into the human race through the woman would reverse that curse of sin. Reversing the curse was good news; in fact, we could call it the gospel!

The sin of Adam spread and intensified. When sin grew worse and reached the point of judgment, God sent the flood to destroy mankind. With the exception of Noah and his family, God eradicated the entire human race. Sinful humanity deserved no less. But destroying the human race was not the promise made to Adam and Eve. Reversing the curse through another human was the promise, but the only humans left on the earth were Noah and his family. There was no Savior in the crowd. The promise to Adam and Eve appeared to be in jeopardy, but God made a covenant with Noah by which He secured and renewed the first promise and disclosed more information. The Lord declared that He would never again destroy the world by flood, thus guaranteeing the continuation of the human race into which the promised Seed, the Savior, was to come. In this progression of gospel revelation, the Lord singled out Noah's son Shem as the progenitor of the specific race into which the Seed would come.[3] The Lord identified the Semitic nations as the specific peoples through whom He would fulfill His promise to reverse the curse. This enlarged truth included the amazing information that God Himself would come into Shem's family line. The Seed would be unique, to say the least.

But once again, sin intensified and earned God's direct intervention. After the rebellion against God at Babel, God scattered and confused the nations, and He called Abraham out of Ur of the Chaldees. The Lord made a covenant with Abraham, a Semite, and the promise became even more specific. God pledged to Abraham that a seed, "the Seed," would come into his line who would bless all the people on earth. By repeating the promise to Isaac and Jacob, God identified the specific Abrahamic line through which the worldwide blessing would come. Interestingly, when Jacob blessed his children before he died, he gave a prophecy that narrowed the lineage of Messiah to the specific tribe of the specific Semitic nation of Israel. The prediction revealed not only that Messiah would come from the tribe of Judah but that He would be a king.

The next incident that more precisely defined the lineage of the Seed occurred about a thousand years later, when God made a covenant with David that the ideal King would be from his family and that He would rule forever. A long time had passed, but God had not forgotten His covenant. Every promise and every seeming delay was making the way ready and increasing the expectancy for Christ. God's covenant revelation concerning Christ progressed generally from the human race to a group of nations to a specific nation to the tribe within the nation to the family in that tribe.

The following illustrates the salient features of the messianic "Seed" identity in successive covenants. The statements are intentionally unabridged to highlight the inherent unity and growth of the revelation. Although the promise to David exhibits more definition than the promise to Adam, the general promise to Adam remains true throughout the development. There is no reason to doubt that the ideal Son to come into David's family is the ideal Man who was promised to Adam's race. Little by little, God made it clear who the Redeemer, the Curse-Reverser, was going to be:

- A Man (Gen. 3:15)
- A Semitic God/Man (Gen. 9:27)
- A Semitic Man from the line of Abraham (Gen. 12, 15, 17)
- A Semitic Man from the line of Isaac from the line of Abraham (Gen. 17:19)
- A Semitic Man from the line of Jacob from the line of Isaac from the line of Abraham (Gen. 26:3, 4)
- A Semitic Man from the tribe of Judah from the line of Jacob from the line of Isaac from the line of Abraham (Gen. 49:10)
- A Semitic Man from the family of David from the tribe of Judah from the line of Jacob from the line of Isaac from the line of Abraham (2 Sam. 7:12–16)

These gracious covenant developments express just one way in which God was directing events toward the fullness of time into which Christ would come. Although the coming of Christ was more than seven hundred years after him and he would not have known that the Redeemer's name would be Jesus of Nazareth, at least in covenant terms Hosea knew as much about the identity of the Redeemer as those alive when Christ did come. The gospel accounts of Christ's birth and identity are in no way startling to those who see the messianic theme in Old Testament covenant revelation; it was part of the agenda of the gospel writers to identify Jesus as the long-awaited covenant promise. Matthew's genealogy of Christ as "the son of David, the son of Abraham" (Matt. 1) and Luke's genealogy, which traces Jesus's human ancestry all the way back to Adam (Luke 3), stand as testimonies to every covenant promise of God. Though the covenant promises moved slowly at times, they always moved steadily, from Eden's paradise to Bethlehem's manger. They had to do so because they were covenant promises that were guaranteed by the oath of God.

All of this revelation antecedent to Hosea must be factored into his creed. What Hosea says about God's making a covenant with the nation (Hos. 2:18) and the nation's breaking the covenant (Hos. 6:7; 8:1) is theologically loaded. It is not hard to find the gospel in Hosea's prophecy when we include in our consideration these core truths about the covenant. Amazingly, with the exception of the Davidic covenant, Hosea knew all of this from Moses. And Moses even anticipated the Davidic covenant when he recorded Israel's last will and testament regarding Judah (Gen. 49:10).

THE IMPLICATIONS OF THE COVENANT

Whereas the covenant installments with Adam, Noah, Abraham, and David identify the person of Christ more and more specifically, the covenant with Israel through Moses explains the work of Christ, His mediatorial ministry—how He would reverse the curse. The exodus from Egypt was Israel's "Independence Day," the birth of a nation. When the people reached Sinai, God entered into a covenant with the nation (Ex. 19). That the exodus began with God's remembering His covenant with Abraham, Isaac, and Jacob (Ex. 2:24) indicates that this covenant at Sinai, marking a decisive point in the exodus journey, was a continuation of the same. The Mosaic covenant is a renewal and expansion of the earlier promises.

Two factors with important gospel implications stand out in the Mosaic covenant: the work of Christ and the condition of faith. In many ways the Mosaic covenant is a theological deliberation in which the Lord explains what the promised Seed must do if He is to reverse the curse and become the worldwide blessing. By all the complex tabernacle operations, the sacrifices, and the ceremonies, God pictured what Christ would do. He was "the Lamb slain from the foundation of the world" (Rev. 13:8) and the substance that cast all the shadows of the Mosaic ritual (Col. 2:17). It is beyond our present scope to catalog all the specific gospel truths latent in the rituals.[4] Suffice it to say that all the ceremonial laws of the Mosaic economy or dispensation were picture prophecies of some aspect of the work of Christ.

The second focus is on the necessary response to the promise of Christ. It is not the fact of Christ that saves. If that were all that was necessary, none would ever perish, since Christ is an indisputable fact. It is the personal appropriation of Christ by faith that saves. The covenant promise of Christ's certain coming and sufficient work is unconditional; nothing could or can frustrate it. But there are conditions for salvation. Personal faith and repentance are requisite for the personal experience of Christ and His work. This is what the Lord sets before the people in Exodus 19:5, a text that is often grossly misinterpreted. The Lord graciously offers them the covenant: "Now therefore, if you will indeed obey My voice and keep My covenant, then you shall be a special treasure to Me above all people. . . ." Unless we impose a completely different definition of the word "covenant"—and there is no warrant for doing so—then obeying this command is tantamount to obeying the gospel. Not obeying the covenant equates with rejecting the message of Christ. Keeping the covenant is believing the gospel. Thus, to agree to the terms of the covenant is far from rejecting its promise; it is accepting grace.

That Moses renewed this covenant at Sinai with the next generation at the threshold of the Promised Land in Deuteronomy emphasizes the necessity of personal appropriation (see Deut. 5:1–3). It also explains why the prophets pressed the same claims on the successive generations (see, for instance, Jer. 11) and why Deuteronomy was so foundational to their theology and their preaching.

Three elements of Deuteronomic theology, in particular, seem to form the outline of Hosea's message to his congregation. At this point I must exercise discipline to resist the temptation to get ahead of myself by discussing Hosea's theology (coming in Part 3) or to fall behind by discussing too much of Deuteronomy. So I'm only going to mention these three elements and wait to see how Hosea parallels them.

Divine Grace

If Moses is clear on anything, it is that God took the initiative in establishing a relationship with Israel (Deut. 10:15). It was all of grace, and nothing of merit. In fact, Moses forthrightly informed the people that they were not to interpret the blessing as a reward of their righteousness, since in reality they were rebellious (Deut. 9:4–6). Deuteronomy 7:6–8 states the grace of God's sovereign election:

> For you are a holy people to the LORD your God; the LORD your God has chosen you to be a people for Himself, a special treasure above all the peoples on the face of the earth. The LORD did not set His love on you nor choose you because you were more in number than any other people, for you were the least of all peoples; but because the LORD loves you.

I love that expression: the Lord loves because He loves (see also Deut. 33:3). The reason for grace is found only within His sovereign will. Grace is at the heart of the gospel. I'll say this much at least: How vividly this grace will be portrayed in Hosea's relationship with Gomer!

Divine Displeasure

Equally clear is God's displeasure—a displeasure precipitated by sin, expressed in judgment, and avoidable by obedience. Moses rehearsed the history of God's consistent dealing with the sins of the wilderness generation (Deut. 9), and he dramatically set before the new generation all the curses that would justly meet their disobedience (Deut. 11:28; 28:15–68) as well as all the blessings that would accompany obedience (Deut. 11:27; 28:1–14). Particularly, the collection of laws in chapters 12–26 defines the specifics of God's covenant terms and expectations, encompassing worship, social relationships, and general behavior in the land. Breaking the covenant had devastating consequences. The Lord threatened drought, disease, defeat, desolation, and deportation from the Promised Land if and when the covenant stipulations were violated.

Interestingly, Moses had said essentially the same things to the old generation (Lev. 26), giving warrant to the prophet's application to future generations. God is always the same. But there was a way to avoid God's displeasure and discipline and thus to remain in the land that was so associated with divine blessing. I suppose in many ways Deuteronomy 27–28, the declaration of covenant curses and blessings, provided the principal antecedent authority for all the prophetic warnings and exhortations—including Hosea's—to repent from all the sins against the covenant, or else. It is not a stretch to see Hosea's references to loss of fertility (Hos. 2:2–13), drought (Hos. 4:3), defeat (Hos. 10:14; 11:6), destruction (Hos. 5:9), and exile (Hos. 8:3; 9:3, 6, 15, 17; 10:6; 11:5; 12:9) as evidences of the predicted divine displeasure. He affirmed his Mosaic theology.

Divine Faithfulness

Finally, Deuteronomy's assurance of God's faithfulness to His promise and to His people warranted every prophetic message of hope. The Lord's covenant was His oath (Deut. 29:12) and therefore certain. What Moses learned of the Lord in his private session in the cloud on the mountain unquestionably affected his final message to the nation:

> The LORD, the LORD God, merciful and gracious, longsuffering, and abounding in goodness and truth, keeping mercy for thousands, forgiving iniquity and transgression and sin, by no means clearing the guilty. (Ex. 34:6–7)

The very character of God explained both the certainty of His displeasure against the guilty and His gracious willingness to forgive those who appeal to His mercy and repent. Just as certainly, therefore, as God threatened death and evil on those who disobeyed the terms of the covenant, so He guaranteed life and good to those who would obey (Deut. 30:11–20). The invitation to choose life and live was not an empty promise (Deut. 30:19). Moses assured his final congregation that it was "not a futile thing" to set their hearts to obey the words of the covenant, because it would be "by this word" that they would prolong their time in the land, the place of blessing (Deut. 32:46–47). Every prophetic invitation to repent and to hope in divine mercy that followed in the years after Moses rested on the same Rock and God of truth (Deut. 32:4).

The bottom line is that Hosea's message cannot be interpreted or fully appreciated in isolation, either historically or theologically. Unquestionably, the corpus of divine revelation that was antecedent to Hosea defined his theological thinking and directed his passionate preaching. Unquestionably, the theology of the covenant framed his ministry. Recognizing the christological content of that gracious covenant, in terms of both its essence and its implications, justifies the claim that Hosea preached the gospel. His creed was Christ. It remains for us to consider the specifics of his message—how and what he preached.

FOR FURTHER REFLECTION

1. Why can Hosea legitimately be called a "Reformed" theologian?
2. Why is the covenant concept so essential to the gospel?
3. Review the major gospel truths pictured in the covenant between God and Israel.
4. How does the nature of progressive revelation substantiate the claim of covenant theology that God has revealed only one way of salvation?

PART TWO

LIFESTYLE EVANGELISM

By divine design, Hosea's life took on "celebrity status"—it was open to public view. It was not unusual for God to instruct His prophets to use object lessons or symbolic acts to illustrate or reinforce some point of their message. But most prophet-performed symbolic acts were occasional and temporary. In contrast to the norm, from the beginning of his prophetic career, Hosea's private life was linked to his public ministry. His entire home life was a picture for all to see, portraying the points of the gospel he was preaching. With words and without a word, Hosea preached and lived the message of God's gracious and constant love for the unlovely. His marriage was symbolic. His personal life pointed to the gospel. That's lifestyle evangelism.

CHAPTER FOUR

A MARRIAGE PORTRAIT

Weddings are happy occasions; marriages are not always so—although they should be. In order to grasp the theological and homiletical consequence of Hosea's tragically unhappy marriage—an integral part of his public ministry—we need to consider the biblical significance of marriage and how the Lord used this special human relationship to picture spiritual truths. There is no more intimate relationship on earth than that between husband and wife. Adam, in his yet sinless state, expressed his understanding of the inseparable connection between himself and the partner God had made especially for him: "This is now bone of my bones and flesh of my flesh" (Gen. 2:23). In his inspired commentary on and application of Adam's statement, Moses made it clear that the marriage bond supersedes every other human connection: "Therefore a man shall leave his father and mother and be joined to his wife, and they shall become one flesh" (Gen. 2:24). It is not surprising that Scripture so frequently uses marriage as the choice symbol of the intimate and everlasting relationship that exists between Christ and His bride, the church.

Interestingly, marriage is not the only human relationship that points to higher spiritual realities. Ironically, some of these relationships appear to be mutually exclusive. For instance, believers are children of God by virtue of both the new birth and adoption. Believers constitute not only the bride of Christ, but also His siblings, for He is the elder brother. In Christ believers are free, but they are also His bond slaves. These opposing analogies raise two issues, one concerning the nature of the gospel and one concerning the nature of analogies. Salvation is wonderfully simple yet profoundly complex: it includes election, regeneration, reconciliation, justification, adoption, sanctification, and more. Salvation is like a chain consisting of several inseparable and unbreakable links. The Scripture sometimes views salvation generally and inclusively of all its constituent parts, and sometimes it specifically focuses on one or another of its components.

Consequently, the life analogies employed by Scripture to help explain salvation vary depending on the particular aspect of the gospel being addressed. Thus, being a child of God by the new birth says something about regeneration, whereas being a child of God by adoption underscores the inviolability of all the legal rights and privileges enjoyed by the redeemed. Both are true, but it takes two mutually exclusive analogies to make the necessary points. Truth trumps analogy. Whereas analogies may appear paradoxical, truth is not. So when the Lord in one place says that He will marry Israel (Hos. 2:19) and then in another refers to Israel as His son (Hos. 11:1), there is no truth contradiction, just different analogies.

The nature of analogy is itself a factor in discovering the point of the truth in focus. The goal of interpretation is to determine the resemblance or point of correspondence between the analogy and the truth, the symbol and reality. Our objective is learning about the truth, not the mechanics of the object lesson. The process of interpreting these analogies is like the mental process required in interpreting most other figures of speech in which comparisons are made between things that share some resemblance. In mental gymnastics, our thoughts swing back and forth between the things being compared in order to determine the appropriate correspondence—what is true about the one that applies to the other. There is usually one main point of correspondence; something about the one resembles and points to the other, but not everything will. Most fanciful interpretations of symbols result from attempts to extract as many points of correspondence as possible. Interpreting figures of speech requires imagination, but an imagination controlled by context.

Here's a simple metaphor to illustrate: the man is a pig. We look at, or at least think about, a pig to learn something about the man—what is true about a pig that applies to the man. The man is not, in fact, a pig, so not everything about a pig is applicable. Depending on the context in which the comparison occurs, it may be the pig's living conditions, eating habits, or size that to some degree describes the man. We do not expect an exhaustive, item-by-item correspondence, but we do assume some point of similarity. Keep this in mind as we consider the message of marriage in Hosea's prophecy. Something about marriage, but not everything, points to the relationship between God and His people. Discovering why so much of Hosea's message revolves around the marriage motif depends on discovering the main point of similarity.

THE LITERAL SIGNIFICANCE OF MARRIAGE

Marriage is significant on many levels. The Westminster Confession of Faith sums up some of the important aspects:

> Marriage is to be between one man and one woman: neither is it lawful for any man to have more than

> one wife, nor for any woman to have more than one husband, at the same time. Marriage was ordained for the mutual help of husband and wife, for the increase of mankind with a legitimate issue, and of the Church with an holy seed; and for preventing of uncleanness. (24.1–2)

Marriage is exclusive; it is for the mutual good of husband and wife; it is the agency for procreation; it is the sphere in which natural sexual desires are to be satisfied. So the Bible declares, "Marriage is honorable among all, and the bed undefiled" (Heb. 13:4). All of this is significant, but not all of it appropriately applies to the ideal spiritual marriage between God and His people, between Christ and His bride the church.

God's institution of marriage and His intent for it frame the theological portrait. From the beginning, marriage was God's idea. The general account of creation declares that God created male and female (Gen. 1:27). The anthropological and covenantal account of creation[1] fills in the specific details of God's logic in creating Eve. It was God's assessment of Adam's estate that it was not good for him to be alone. So with self-determination and personal interest[2] God pronounced His resolve: "I will make a helper comparable to him" (Gen. 2:18). God's parading all the animals of paradise before Adam was enough to convince him of the accuracy of God's assessment and to create eagerness for God's solution (Gen. 2:19–20). When Adam awoke from his surgery, he expressed his satisfaction with what he saw. Before his divinely induced sleep, he saw the procession of creatures over which he was to have dominion but with which he could not enjoy companionship. After his sleep, his eyes fell on woman, and he exclaimed, "Now we're talking!" At least, that's my dynamically equivalent translation of his description of the one God had just formed from his own body to be comparable to him: "This is now bone of my bones and flesh of my flesh" (Gen. 2:23). Adam immediately recognized one created to be his equal and not just another in the long line of creatures over which he was to have preeminence (Gen. 1:26). This marked the beginning of a special relationship.

God's intent in instituting this relationship was manifold. In the institution of marriage God provided the means for meeting pre-fallen man's needs for companionship (Gen. 2:18), romance (Gen. 2:24–25), and reproduction (Gen. 1:28). Those needs continued after the fall, and although sin tended to pervert the relationship, marriage continued to serve the intended purposes. Notwithstanding the importance of these marriage principles, the fact that God initiated marriage in covenant terms is at the heart of its theological significance and is key to understanding Hosea's use of the marriage theme. Marriage as a covenant, then, is the principal point of correspondence for the spiritual analogy.

Although the actual word for covenant (*berith*) rarely designates the marriage bond in the Old Testament (see Ezek. 16:8 and Mal. 2:14), the evidence of a covenant exists. The adage about ducks is applicable here. If it looks like a duck and walks like a duck and quacks like a duck, it most likely is a duck. Covenant terminology and circumstances attendant with covenants are common. Remember that we have defined a covenant as a mutually binding agreement between two parties. In marriage, there are two parties; there are terms of agreement; there are promises and obligations. It looks like a covenant, and thanks to Malachi's direct statement, we know it is.

Moses sets the covenant context for marriage in his inspired comment on Adam's "love-at-first-sight" statement regarding his newly created counterpart: "Therefore a man shall leave his father and mother and be joined to his wife, and they shall become one flesh" (Gen. 2:24). Marriage exists when a man leaves his childhood supervision, unites with his wife in a new and exclusive relationship, and intimately and indissolubly becomes one with her. Unquestionably, becoming one flesh is a euphemism for sexual union (see 1 Cor. 6:16), but it has far greater consequence. That it designates the divinely intended permanence of relationship between the two covenanting parties is clear from Christ's comment on the statement: "Therefore what God has joined together, let not man separate" (Matt. 19:6). Confirming the covenant connection are the verbs Moses used that in later contexts find function in the spiritual sphere. The verbs "to leave" (*'zb*) and "to be joined" (*dbq*) elsewhere designate spiritual and covenantal transactions. Leaving sometimes describes the covenant violation of forsaking the Lord (e.g., Hos. 4:10; Jer. 1:16) whereas being joined positively describes clinging to the Lord (e.g., Deut. 10:20; 11:22; 13:4). The imageries of abandoning one relationship for another and cleaving to a person in a new relationship find definition in the first marriage, which lays the lexical foundation for the covenant usage of the words in subsequent contexts. In ensuing texts, "leaving" usually has negative tones of forsaking the Lord, whereas "cleaving" usually specifies allegiance to God. The point is that both words are part of covenant jargon.

In the covenant of marriage, a husband and a wife pledge their exclusive allegiance to each other. Marriage is to be monogamous: one man and one woman. The first marriage set the paradigm for monogamy, but the perversion of polygamy soon distorted the institution and its purpose by reducing the woman to either a tool for procreation or property for male satisfaction. But monogamy was God's intent, and the kind of thrill Adam expressed over Eve is still attainable notwithstanding sin's influence: "Live joyfully with the wife whom you love all the days of your vain life . . ." (Eccl. 9:9). The Song of Solomon details the beauty, dignity, and sanctity of marriage, the most precious of human love relationships. Regardless of the interpretation difficulties in the Song, one thing is remarkably clear: the couple expressed exclusive love and loyalty to each other. In fact, they just could not get over each other; they were the two sole members of a mutual admiration society.

That marriage is an exclusive covenant relationship is why adultery is such a heinous sin. Not only does it involve fornication, but it violates a sacred covenant bond between the husband and wife. Adultery is unfaithfulness and disloyalty to a binding agreement, to a covenant. The marriage contract is not to be violated. Malachi's condemnation of divorce covers any breach of the marriage contract: ". . . she is your companion and your wife by covenant . . . let none deal treacherously with the wife of his youth" (Mal. 2:14–15). So once again, the fact that marriage is a covenant not to be broken is what constitutes the principal point of correspondence in its use as an analogy for spiritual truth.

THE SYMBOLIC FUNCTION OF MARRIAGE

Throughout the Old Testament, marriage is a symbol or object lesson of God's relationship with His people. Not surprisingly, Moses first employed the analogy, principally with lexical allusions; the prophets, beginning with Hosea, used the image extensively to illustrate some point in their sermons. Since the concept of covenant is such a prominent component in theological truth, it is fitting that marriage—the most personal and intimate of human covenants—should be used by the inspired authors to illustrate the nature, terms, and expectations of that covenant between God and the people He had chosen to be His own.

The next chapter will detail the use of the symbol in Hosea, so at this juncture I want simply to highlight some of the other places and ways the image occurs in the Old

Testament. Hosea's audience had no excuse for not getting his point.

First, the marriage analogy helps to put God's jealousy in perspective. Significantly, in one of the most important covenant declarations to the newly constituted nation of Israel, God warned the people against worshipping any other god and gave reason for the warning with this Self-revelation: "for the LORD, whose name is Jealous, is a jealous God" (Ex. 34:14). His jealousy demanded their exclusive allegiance, just as a husband or wife would have every right to expect exclusive faithfulness from a spouse. Moses invariably refers to God's jealousy in terms of covenant requirements (e.g. Ex. 20:6; Deut. 4:24; 5:6; 6:15).

Admittedly, *jealousy* is a loaded word, often connoting negative notions of pettiness, paranoia, or covetousness. However, the fact that the concept applies to God must mean that it's not all bad: "For the LORD is righteous, He loves righteousness . . ." (Ps. 11:7). Everything about God and everything He does always agree with who He is. So God's jealousy is a manifestation of His infinite holiness. The Hebrew root *qn'* (occurring in noun, adjective, and verb forms) denotes deep emotion and ardent zeal. It effectively describes God's intense passion[3] for His own name, His word, and His people. The prophet Zechariah recorded explicitly God's declaration of jealousy for His people: "I am zealous for Jerusalem and for Zion with great zeal" (Zech. 1:14). That zealous fervor necessarily translates into appropriate actions to safeguard the object of ardor. Jealousy is a zealous vigilance that is inflexibly intolerant of any rivalry. God's jealousy is both a warning against violating the covenant and an encouragement that God will protect His own.

Consequently, it is not unexpected that this word would have a marriage connection. The test for unfaithfulness in Numbers 5:11–31, notwithstanding its enigmatic procedures for determining guilt, clearly connects jealousy to marriage. Although the husband may be guilty of undue suspicion and petty insecurity, he nonetheless has a legitimate interest in insuring and protecting the exclusiveness of the relationship with his wife (see also Prov. 6:34). Significantly, the inspired Song extolling all the virtues of marriage links love and jealousy (Song 8:6). The imagery comparing love to death and jealousy to the grave and fire may appear strange, but the point of the comparison is clear enough: the emotions are inevitable and enduring. Thus, to define God's jealousy as suspicious envy would be ludicrously blasphemous, whereas to regard it as His deep-seated, exclusive, and ardent passion that governs His vital interest in what inherently or covenantally belongs to Him is certainly not. The jealousy of God rightfully demands the exclusive allegiance of those who by covenant belong to Him and puts into action His determination to vouchsafe the sanctity of what is His. Even though the human marriage relationship may at times trivialize or distort the legitimate and proper expressions of jealousy, it nonetheless sets a framework for our understanding God's righteous jealousy and His demands in light of it.

Second, the marriage analogy puts Israel's apostasy in perspective. The marriage bond assumes, indeed demands, that there be an exclusive union between husband and wife that must be maintained and guarded. Adultery is the violation of that bond and is a most serious and grievous offense both against the spouse and against God (Ex. 20:14). The prohibition not even to covet another's wife (Ex. 20:17) insures that the sanctity and exclusiveness of the marriage relationship includes the issues of the heart, not just the flesh (see Matt. 5:28). Faithfulness and mutual loyalty between husband and wife are basic to marriage. Unfaithfulness and disloyalty threaten and jeopardize the union. Not surprisingly, then, Israel's forsaking the Lord is often described in terms of harlotry or spiritual adultery—a tragically vivid picture of apostasy.

The same covenant text that declared the Lord's name as Jealous warns against worshipping other gods and adds the explanation that such action would be participation in harlotry (Ex. 34:14–16). Using the marriage imagery, Jeremiah sums up Israel's apostasy and its consequences with vivid language:

> Have you seen what backsliding Israel has done? She has gone up on every high mountain and under every green tree, and there played the harlot. . . . Then I saw that for all the causes for which backsliding Israel had committed adultery, I had put her away and given her a certificate of divorce; yet her treacherous sister Judah did not fear, but went and played the harlot also. So it came to pass, through her casual harlotry, that she defiled the land and committed adultery with stones and trees. (Jer. 3:6–9)

Similarly, Ezekiel's allegory of the foundling-turned-wife describes the breaking of the marriage covenant between the Lord and Israel in graphic terms of harlotry (Ezek. 16:16–34). Ezekiel 16:32 says all that is necessary: "You are an adulterous wife, who takes strangers instead of her husband." Ezekiel's parable of the two sisters Oholah and Oholibah—representing Samaria and Jerusalem—in shocking terms defines their sin as harlotry (Ezek. 23). Hosea's use of this symbol is all the more weighty since Hosea lives it before the people; his portrait of marriage was more than allegory. More about this is coming.

THE TYPICAL REALIZATION OF MARRIAGE

Not only was the marriage covenant a fitting object lesson or symbol of significant spiritual truths in the Old Testament, but it was also a type or picture prophecy of redemptive truths that found fulfillment in Jesus Christ and His special, intimate, unique relationship with the church, His bride. Factoring in the typical realization of marriage, therefore, increases the gospel implications of Hosea's message. Thinking about the most precious of human love relationships points to that love that supersedes all human love. Even the failures of the human relationship contribute to the anticipation for the ideal; with this notion in view, Hosea's contribution to messianic expectancy is immense.

Psalm 45 provides outstanding evidence of the Old Testament's use of marriage as typical or prophetic of Christ. This is a royal psalm—a psalm dealing with some aspect of kingship—celebrating the royal wedding. That Hebrews 1:8 quotes verses six and seven as referring specifically to Christ suggests the conclusion that this psalm has at least some messianic reference.[4] The inspired poet-prophet typically employs the marriage theme to spotlight the beauty of the spiritual union between the coming Christ and His people. It is not surprising that he begins the predictive poem with his confession, "My heart is overflowing with a good theme" (Ps. 45:1), and ends with his assurance that "the people shall praise You [the King] forever and ever" (Ps. 45:17). In between, the psalm describes the King's beauty, His might, His throne, and His merit. The royal husband is precious to His bride; He protects and defends His bride; He rules for the welfare of His bride; He shares His wealth and merit with His bride. This is not the place to expound the psalm, but needless to say, it draws lines directly to Christ and the gospel. It is my opinion that the only difference between understanding this text in the old dispensation versus the new is that we know the King's name is Jesus. God intended for them then and for us now to see in this wedding song what belongs to believers in union with Christ—a prophecy in portrait.

Types do not necessarily depend on explicit New Testament verification, but New Testament corroboration removes any doubt about identifying Old Testament types. Two New Testament passages stand out as verifying the link between marriage and Christ's relationship to the church. Notably, Revelation 19 describes the indissoluble union between Christ and His people in the eternal state in terms of marriage: "Let us be glad and rejoice and give Him glory, for the marriage of the Lamb has come, and His wife has made herself ready. And to her it was granted to be arrayed in fine linen, clean and bright, for the fine linen is the righteous acts of the saints. . . . Blessed are those who are called to the marriage supper of the Lamb . . ." (Rev. 19:7–9). This marriage supper represents the consummation of what Paul intended for Corinthian believers and by extension for all believers: "For I have betrothed you to one husband, that I may present you as a chaste virgin to Christ" (2 Cor. 11:2). The imagery reflects the Near Eastern custom of arranged marriages in which the father chose the bride and by which a betrothal declared publicly the covenant union between a man and woman that established them legally as husband and wife.[5] Following this betrothal period, the groom would take the bride from her home to his for celebration and cohabitation. So in the spiritual parallel, the Father chose a bride for His Son, and the Holy Spirit established the covenant union between that bride and Christ, sealing to the bride all the benefits of grace. All that remains is for Christ to come for His bride and to take her home to be with Him forever in that blessed place where there is no death to cause a parting. Union with Christ is good now, but the best is yet to be, and it is to be forever.

Hosea's love for undeserving Gomer was to be according to God's love for undeserving Israel (Hos. 3:1). Marriage is a legally binding covenant, but it is also a bond of love. Significantly, the most extensive New Testament text comparing Christ's relationship with the church to marriage highlights the theme of love (Eph. 5:22–33). Husbands are to love their wives as Christ loves His church; Christ's love for the church sets the ideal standard for every husband's love for his wife. Obviously, no mere man can attain perfect Christlikeness, but the closer married love approximates the ideal, the better the marriage will be. Christlike love is selfless, sacrificial, and special. Christ gave Himself for the church He loved. His love was not mere talk; He proved it in all the appropriate acts necessary to procure and protect His bride. Paul explains the special union that the church has with Christ in marriage language: "For we are members of His body, of His flesh and of His bones" (Eph. 5:30). This intimate spiritual union is a mystery (Eph. 5:32)—something that would be too bold to think or seemingly too good to be true apart from God's revelation. But God has revealed it to be true, and it remains for us to see marriage for all of its gospel worth. The comment of Charles Hodge regarding this passage sums it well: "Paul . . . in Ephesians 5:22–33, represents marriage as a most ennobling spiritual union; which raises man out of himself and makes him live for another. . . . Marriage . . . does for man in the sphere of nature, what union with Christ does for him in the sphere of grace."[6]

The bottom line is that God has made marriage a choice symbol of His own relationship with His people. The spiritual parallel lifts family life to a high and significant plane. The love of Christ for His people regulates and defines the love the husband should show his wife; and loyalty of the church to Christ indicates the faithful loyalty the wife should show to her husband. Christian husbands and wives owe to Christ the purification of their relations and the sanctification of their homes. God ordained marriage for the lifelong companionship, help, and comfort which husband and wife ought to have for each other. In the covenant of marriage both husband and wife must commit themselves to each other completely in compassion and understanding. Marriage is a covenant of faith and trust between a man and a woman, a covenant of hope that endures all things, a covenant of love in which both husband and wife empty themselves of self and their own concerns and esteem each other more highly than themselves. It is not surprising that God so often uses marriage to communicate spiritual truths to His people. Indeed, a good marriage that fulfills all the requirements of love and loyalty becomes a never-ending sermon of the gospel itself. However, a marriage that fails is tragic; it has turned out contrary to expectation, but it is nonetheless spiritually instructive. One way or another, there is always a message in marriage. The marriage portrait helps to put Hosea in perspective.

FOR FURTHER REFLECTION

1. How can Christians be the bride of Christ, children of God by a new birth, and children of God by adoption, all at once?
2. Why should every Christian marriage be a living gospel sermon?
3. When is jealousy appropriate?

CHAPTER FIVE

UP CLOSE AND PERSONAL

The message of marriage is an integral part of the prophecy of Hosea. Whereas most prophecies begin with some command for the prophet to prophesy, Hosea begins with the Lord's instruction for him to get married. God intended Hosea's family life to be a symbol, a visible picture or object lesson, of the message he was to preach to Israel. Hosea 3:1, the key verse of the prophecy, explicitly links Hosea's marriage to Gomer with God's marriage to Israel: "love a woman . . . just like the love of the LORD for the children of Israel. . . ." It was not unusual for the Lord to instruct His prophets to use some symbolic act to accompany a part of the message. Sometimes those symbolic acts would cause embarrassment, such as when Isaiah walked around naked and barefoot (Isa. 20) or Jeremiah walked around with a yoke around his neck (Jer. 27). Sometimes the symbolic act would cause significant inconvenience, such as when Jeremiah traveled back and forth to the Euphrates with the linen sash (Jer. 13). Sometimes the symbolic act might even cause some temporary discomfort, such as when Ezekiel lay on his right and left sides for prolonged periods (Ezek. 4). But Hosea was unique in that his whole life was symbolic, an object lesson of what he would preach. Any who saw or knew about

Hosea's ordeal could only feel sorry for him. The Lord was using his whole miserable, tragic experience of personal sorrow and emotional distress to portray a vivid lesson to Israel. Hosea's constant love and loyalty to Gomer was a beautiful picture of the Lord's unfailing love and loyalty to Israel. Gomer's unfaithfulness to Hosea was a tragically clear picture of Israel's treacherous unfaithfulness to the Lord. Therefore, properly understanding Hosea's marriage to Gomer is vital to understanding the message of his prophecy, and understanding the message gives some insight for properly interpreting his marriage.

To miss the connection between Hosea's marriage to Gomer and the Lord's marriage to Israel is to miss the obvious. Although many in the nation were deaf to Hosea's preaching, even the dullest of them could see Hosea's grief, sympathize with his sorrow, and wonder at his persistent love.[1] Hosea's home life became a living sermon: Hosea's was "lifestyle" evangelism in the most appropriate sense. Humanly speaking, Hosea's love for Gomer did not make any sense. But that is the very point of the message: God's love for sinners does not make any sense apart from His free and sovereign grace. So looking at Hosea up close and personal will mirror something about the gospel.

THE PROBLEM WITH THE MARRIAGE

We can identify the problem quickly and briefly. The crux of the problem of Hosea's marriage to Gomer is very much on the surface and right at the beginning of book. The conundrum concerns the initial command that God gave to the prophet: "Go, take yourself a wife of harlotry [a]nd children of harlotry" (Hos. 1:2). On the surface this creates a moral and ethical dilemma because it seems to counter the clear instruction and restrictions for marriage that God gave to others employed in His service. In Leviticus 21:7, for instance, the Lord prohibits priests from marrying a harlot: "They shall not take a wife who is a harlot or a defiled woman . . . for the priest is holy to his God." The Lord further specified that the high priest had to marry "a wife in her virginity" (Lev. 21:13). Although priests and prophets performed distinct functions, they both served in mediatorial and messianic capacities. The priest represented the people before God; the prophet represented God before the people. If it would be a disgrace for a priest to marry a harlot, it would seem to follow that it would be a disgrace for a prophet as well.

Not only is this restriction in view for public figures, but Deuteronomy 22:20–21 sentences any woman to death by stoning if proven to be unchaste at the time of her marriage—no matter whom she was going to marry (Deut. 22:13). In light of this paradigm, it would seem that Hosea should begin with a funeral service rather than a wedding ceremony. The dilemma, therefore, is twofold: Would the Lord lower the standards of marriage for a prophet, who stood as His representative, and would He arbitrarily overlook the impurity and pardon from the prescribed penalty this "wife of harlotry"? Virtually all agree this is the problem.

PROPOSED SOLUTIONS TO THE PROBLEM

Solving the problem is not as simple as stating it. The proposed solutions to this problem have been many. The solutions fall into two major categories: those that regard the marriage as hypothetical and those that regard the marriage as literal. Although it is not necessary in this venue to discuss the differing views in detail,[2] a summary identification and evaluation of the standard interpretations is in order to justify my argument for an actual marriage between Hosea and Gomer. Notwithstanding the problem and opposing solutions, the function of marriage in Hosea's message is indisputable. As Longman and Dillard succinctly conclude, "Hosea's marriage with Gomer (whether historical, symbolic, allegorical, or visionary) is used by God to indicate both his disgust with and his love for his covenant people."[3]

Hypothetical Marriage

The hypothetical view denies a real historical marriage between Hosea and Gomer and interprets Hosea's use of the marriage imagery as simply a means of communicating figuratively God's relationship to Israel and Israel's spiritual unfaithfulness to God. Those espousing this view generally argue that an actual marriage would have reflected poorly on God's holiness and would have greatly hindered Hosea's ministry. Calvin contends that an actual marriage with an impure woman would have disqualified the prophet from any kind of ministry: "how could he expect to be received . . . after having brought on himself such a disgrace?"[4] E. J. Young compares Hosea's being involved with an impure woman with a Christian minister's becoming "entangled with a woman of loose character" and concludes that both men would have been rendered ineffective for ministry before their respective congregations.[5] Keil furthermore objects to an actual marriage on the basis of God's character, claiming the whole situation "would be quite irreconcilable with the holiness of God . . . since God, as the Holy One, cannot possibly sanction adultery."[6]

According to this view, the best way to resolve the moral and theological tension is to disallow the fact but not the significance of the marriage. The marriage conveyed a message even if there were no actual nuptials. It is as though Hosea introduced his ministry with a "what if." Calvin explains it this way and claims to see "nothing strained in this explanation":

> When, therefore, the Prophet began to teach, he commenced somewhat in this way: "The Lord places me here as on a stage, to make known to you that I have married a wife, a wife habituated to adulteries and whoredoms, and that I have begotten children by her." The whole people knew that he had done no such thing; but the Prophet spake thus in order to set before their eyes a vivid representation. Such, then, was the vision . . . that the people might see, as in a living portraiture, their turpitude and perfidiousness. It is, in short, an exhibition, in which the thing itself is not only set forth in words, but is also placed, as it were, before their eyes in a visible form.[7]

Young, similarly, says that the entire scenario is symbolic and that the prophet is conveying to the people what God revealed to him.[8] Keil, however, is cautious not to diminish the sense of heartache Hosea would have felt as this episode played out internally in his spiritual consciousness. What he recited to the people really happened; it just happened inside, not outside: "The inward experience has quite as much reality and truth as the outward; whereas a parable or a poetical fiction has simply a certain truth, so far as the subjective imagination is concerned, but no reality."[9]

The hypothetical interpretation thus has the advantage of avoiding the moral, ethical, and practical problems associated with an actual marriage while still allowing the marriage motif to make the theological point regarding God's love for an undeserving people. But despite Calvin's self-defense against strained exegesis, the weakness of the view is that it seems to be forced by theological expediency rather than textual evidence. In reality, there seems to be nothing in the text to suggest symbolic language. It appear to be straightforward historical narrative that includes seemingly mundane data with no symbolic significance apart from what might be conceived by a fertile imagination.[10] For instance, the weaning of Lo-Ruhamah (Hos. 1:8) seems to be a narrative detail without any obvious spiritual significance. The absence of terminology often used to introduce prophetic visions (*r'h* or *khzh*) also points to a literal occurrence.

Literal Marriage

There are several versions of the actual marriage interpretation, all agreeing that a real marriage took place but disagreeing on the nature or timing of the harlotry ascribed to Gomer. The views can be summed up in four categories. I'll spend the most time explaining mine.

First, the *harlot view* maintains that Gomer was in fact impure, perhaps a temple prostitute, when Hosea married her. Those holding this view recognize the moral difficulty but suggest that for the sake of the message, God overruled His previously stated standards.[11] Hosea's marrying the harlot would emphasize God's gracious love for an undeserving people. Gomer's continuing adultery was an affront to Hosea's kindness as Israel's was to God's.

Second, the *idolatress view* claims that Gomer was an idol worshipper when she married Hosea. The word *harlotry* would then refer to spiritual rather than sexual fornication.[12] Although this eliminates the surface problem of the prophet's marriage to a sexually unchaste woman, it creates a no-less-serious problem if the Lord commanded the prophet to marry a blatant unbeliever. The principal intent of the Lord's prohibition for the people not to intermarry with the Canaanites was to maintain not ethnic separation but religious separation (Deut. 7:3–4; Ex. 34:15–16). It parallels the New Testament demand that marriage be "in the Lord" (1 Cor. 7:39). In addition, if Gomer's harlotry was only spiritual, the details concerning the birth of the three children have no direct significance. Although it is not stated unequivocally, there may be a tacit hint that

Hosea was not the father of two of the children. Whereas concerning Jezreel the text says that Gomer "bore him" a son (Hos. 1:3), the reference to "him" or Hosea is missing from the statements concerning Lo-Ruhamah and Lo-Ammi (Hos. 1:6, 8). Admittedly, not all interpreters see significance in the different wording, and other texts referring to unquestionably legitimate births make no reference to the father (see, for instance, 1 Sam. 1:20), but to me the contrast seems intentional. So if, indeed, the absence of that statement is significant, it would suggest that Gomer's sin was more than idolatry.

Third, the *proleptic view* claims that Gomer was sexually pure at the beginning of the marriage but soon became unfaithful. Prolepsis is the use of a descriptive word in anticipation of a later occurrence that will make the term appropriate. Accordingly, though pure at marriage, Gomer was identified as a "wife of harlotry" in anticipation of what she would become. God, who knows the end from the beginning, could certainly reveal to Hosea what his bride would do before she actually committed acts of fornication. Proponents of this view usually argue that Hosea wrote this prophecy toward the end of his lengthy prophetic career after the events had transpired. Writing these chapters as history, he naturally would use language reflecting what he later discovered.[13] It would be similar to my relating an incident involving my wife when she was a young child and in the process referring to her as my wife. She was not my wife then, but because she now is I could speak in those terms. God told Hosea to marry Gomer; when she proved to be unfaithful, Hosea could say that God told him to marry an immoral person. This maintains Gomer's initial purity and avoids the violation of the legislation from the Pentateuch. This view is widely held and is attractive to me as a viable answer. However, although this interpretation has advantages, it does not do justice to the exact wording of Hosea 1:2. As Hosea records it, the text is a direct quotation of what the Lord commanded at the beginning of his ministry: what Gomer was, not what she would be.

Although all of these proposed solutions attempt to address the problem, they seem either to ignore part of the evidence or to create a new set of difficulties. There is a fourth and simpler solution that avoids the obvious moral and ethical dilemma (the advantage of the proleptic view) while maintaining the wording of the text as the direct words of the Lord to Hosea at the beginning of his prophetic career (avoiding the principal weakness of the proleptic view). I'm not sure what to call this fourth view. For now, I'll refer to it as the *hybrid view*: a cross between the harlot view that takes the initial command at face value and the proleptic view that postpones Gomer's infidelity.

The answer may be in the significance of the word translated "harlotry" (*zenunim*). Although the word relates to the root word for prostitution and may apply to an act of prostitution (see Gen. 38:24), it is not the word that normally designates a prostitute. It is an abstract plural that would more likely describe an inner characteristic than an outward behavior.[14] It most likely refers to Gomer's latent bent toward immorality that surfaced not long after the marriage. God revealed to Hosea upfront something about Gomer's inner self that would potentially jeopardize the sanctity of the marriage. God allowed Hosea to see Gomer in a way that otherwise only He could see: "For the LORD does not see as man sees; for man looks at the outward appearance, but the LORD looks at the heart" (1 Sam. 16:7). At the beginning of the marriage she was innocent of any physical fornication, but Hosea knew both what she was capable of doing and what she most likely would do. It was just a matter of time before propensity became practice.

In many ways, Gomer was a child of her times.[15] Baal worship had become widespread, along with its sexual promiscuity. Baal was a fertility god: immorality played a prominent part in the cultic rituals. Such immorality, sponsored by the false priests and prophets and practiced in the name of religion, contributed to loose living throughout society. Everywhere Gomer would look there were evidences of sexual license, and tragically, there was something in her that answered to what she saw. She had the world in her heart and ultimately gave way to that propensity to immorality. Her being described as an adulterous woman in Hosea 3:1 indicates that her inclinations indeed surfaced in outright fornication. She became what she thought about, for thinking always determines behavior. That the word translated "committing adultery" (*mena'afeth*) in Hosea 3:1 is a Piel participle suggests that she became completely enslaved to the licentious behavior.[16]

This "hybrid" interpretation has the marked advantage of viewing Hosea 1:2 as a direct quotation of God's initial command to Hosea. Though in practice innocent at the time of marriage, Gomer was inwardly biased toward promiscuity. Because she was outwardly pure at the beginning of the marriage, she would not have been a hindrance to Hosea's acceptance or effectiveness as a prophet. That Hosea knew from the Lord's instruction her potential for hurting him highlighted the unselfish nature of his love. This is a key link to the spiritual parallel: God loves us in spite of what He knows about us.

This definition of *zenunim* also explains the phrase "take . . . children of harlotry" (Hos. 1:2). This does not mean that Gomer already had children when Hosea married her.[17] This is a literary device called *zeugma*. Zeugma occurs when a single verb grammatically governs two nouns although it logically controls only one. An implicit verb governs the other noun and must be supplied to give the full sense. Here's a simple example: "I heard the thunder and lightning." Since lightning is seen rather than heard, the full statement would be "I heard the thunder and saw the lightning." The elliptical statement is clear enough. Thus, the statement "take yourself a wife of harlotry and children of harlotry" means take a wife and *have* children. These children, like their mother, were characterized by *zenunim*. Therefore, this qualifying description of the children does not mean that they were born in fornication. In fact, I have already indicated that while I believe Lo-Ruhamah and Lo-Ammi were born from an illicit affair, Jezreel was legitimately Hosea's son. Nonetheless, he shared the same epithet with his siblings: children of harlotry. The idea is that they had an inner bent to evil that made them susceptible to contamination by their environment—just as their mother was. Potentially wayward children only added to the heartbreak of Hosea's home life.

PARALLELS WITH THE MESSAGE

Knowing how to look at Hosea's life up close and personal helps us to know what we should be focusing on. Each of the proposed solutions to Hosea's problematic marriage agrees on the big picture: the relationship of Hosea, Gomer, and the three children illustrates something about God's grace to an undeserving people. Hosea's home life was a showcase for the gospel and its implications.

Here is the snapshot of Hosea's marriage that will shape my analysis of his message. Gomer was outwardly pure when Hosea married her, but being inwardly inclined to promiscuity, she potentially threatened the success and sanctity of the marriage. Hosea and Gomer together started a family: Gomer bore a son to Hosea. Sometime after the birth of Jezreel, Gomer succumbed to her latent desires and gave birth to two more children as the result of adulterous affairs. What started as a happy home ended in tragic sadness. This is how I suggest looking broadly at Hosea's life; now here is what I want us specifically to see.

Interestingly, at every major event in the recorded family history (the marriage, the birth of the children, and the separation and reunion), the Lord specifies the salient spiritual lesson He all along intended to depict through Hosea's experience. In Part 3 I will develop the principal theological themes that sum up God's relationship with Israel under three main thoughts: It was a relationship initiated by love, spurned by sin, and maintained by loyalty. Significantly, Hosea's relationship with Gomer points up the same three themes: he loved her, he was rejected by her, and he took her back. Hosea 2 draws a straight line from Gomer to Israel: Israel's sin mirrors Gomer's adultery (2:2–5); and Israel's judgment mirrors Gomer's degradation and separation from Hosea (2:6–11); and Israel's ultimate restoration to blessing mirrors Gomer's reunion with Hosea (2:14–23). So on several levels, Hosea's experience parallels God's relationship with Israel, which in turn is paradigmatic of God's salvific acts for the church. The gospel pervades both Hosea's life and his message.

The Message of Gomer

God appended this explanation to His command for Hosea to marry Gomer: "For the land has committed great harlotry by departing from the Lord" (Hos. 1:2). Thus, the Lord gives the first clue that there is going to be something spiritually symbolic about Hosea's relationship with Gomer. If Gomer was indeed morally pure at the inception of her relationship with Hosea, then that initial innocence ought to find some correspondence with the spiritual reality. There is, in fact, evidence to warrant this parallel. The fact that God charges the nation with departing from Him suggests that at one point they were with Him. Jeremiah, years later, referred to the former condition of the nation with these words from the Lord: "I remember you, the kindness of your youth, the love of your betrothal. . . . Israel was holiness to the Lord" (Jer. 2:2–3). Likewise, Hosea 2:15

anticipates the future restoration of the people in a way that suggests a previous state of blessing: "She shall sing there, as in the days of her youth, as in the day when she came up from the land of Egypt." According to this predicted restitution, the exodus event marked the spiritual ideal. This event that gave birth to the nation led to God's entering into covenant with the nation (Ex. 19:5–6) and was accompanied by Israel's commitment to that covenant. The new nation entered the covenant with a resolute pledge, a collective "I do": "All that the Lord has spoken we will do" (Ex. 19:8). To use the image before us, this was the wedding day—a solemn but happy occasion with immense potential for blessing.

So despite the insight into Gomer's character and the consequent foresight of what Gomer would potentially do, Hosea most likely entered the marriage with expectancy that his love would win Gomer's affection and make him irresistibly attractive to her regardless of her secret passions. But the happy hope was short-lived. It was not long before Gomer put Hosea out of sight and yielded to whoever tempted her to stray. She conceived children illicitly and degenerated into a promiscuous and adulterous lifestyle. Neither did it take long for Israel to reveal its latent idolatrous heart. As soon as Moses was out of sight, the people erected the golden calf (Ex. 32), and things got worse as time went on.

Do not miss the gospel lesson pictured here. Hosea loved Gomer in spite of what he knew about her, in spite of the potential of his being deeply hurt by her. The Scripture gives no hint regarding Gomer's outward appearance; it does, however, reveal the blackness of her heart. But even if she was physically attractive, her inward character was so repulsive that loving her made no sense. As amazing as Hosea's love for Gomer was, it pales in comparison to God's love for us. Listen to how Paul puts it: "But God demonstrates His own love toward us, in that while we were still sinners, Christ died for us" (Rom. 5:8). Again the apostle says, "But God, who is rich in mercy, because of His great love with which He loved us, even when we were dead in trespasses, made us alive together with Christ (by grace you have been saved)" (Eph. 2:4–5). God knows us for what we really are, and there is nothing about us that is appealing or attractive. On the contrary, our sin is disgusting before Him (see, for instance, Isa. 59:2; 64:6). But He loves us in spite of our sin. And what is more, He freely loves us knowing that our love to Him will be imperfect and that in one way or another we will be unfaithful. His loving us does not depend on how well or much we love Him in return; His love for us is sovereignly gracious. Even more so, remember that Hosea, the prophet, was a type of Christ, the ideal Prophet. If Hosea's unselfish love for Gomer symbolizes generally God's gracious love for His people, it typifies specifically Christ's self-sacrificing love for His church. Therefore, as disgusting as Gomer may appear, every Christian must admit the Gomer that is his or her own heart. Admitting that Gomer-like heart, every Christian should offer praise and thanksgiving for sovereign and saving grace. Amazing grace! Amazing love!

Once again the Lord Himself draws the line between Hosea's act and His: "Go again, love a woman who is loved by a lover and is committing adultery, just like the love of the LORD for the children of Israel, who look to other gods . . . " (Hos. 3:1). Although the narrative does not specify any kind of separation between Hosea and Gomer after her trysts, the Lord's command in chapter 3 implies that some kind of separation had occurred, and the application to Israel in chapter 2 detailing a separation and restoration assumes a parallel to Hosea's experience. Consequently, not only does Hosea's loving Gomer in spite of his knowing her true character anticipate gospel grace, but his taking her back after her wayward adultery symbolizes God's forgiving and unfailing love for His sinning people. Confessedly, some of the details in Hosea 3 are problematic. Some even question whether Hosea 3:1 refers to Gomer.[18] But to see someone other than Gomer raises more questions than it answers and does not correspond well with the obvious spiritual parallel that God restores wayward Israel to Himself.

The identity of the lover of the woman is also open for speculation. The Hebrew text literally says, "a woman loved of a friend." The question is whether the friend refers to Hosea or to one of Gomer's paramours. In Song of Solomon 5:16 the word designates the legitimate spouse: "This is my beloved, and this is my friend." Yet in Jeremiah 3:1 it refers to those with whom Israel had played the harlot. Context must determine the referent, and here the context is inconclusive. Although I cannot prove it, I believe the reference is to Hosea. In spite of all Gomer had done against him, his love for her remained constant. He did not stop loving her even though she had wronged him and hurt him deeply. I like the spiritual parallel this suggests regarding God's love for His people.

Verses 2 and 3 pose some problems as well. Verse 2 stipulates the price he paid for Gomer but does not identify whom he paid or why he paid the stated amount. Some speculate that because the price, fifteen shekels, approximates the stated value of a slave (Ex. 21:32), Gomer had become the property of one of her illicit lovers. Others relate what happened here to the episode recorded in Judges 19:1–3 and argue that Gomer, like the immoral concubine in that narrative, returned to her father's house. The ambiguity of the text seems to indicate that who received the payment and the exact amount of the payment are incidental. The point is that Hosea did what was necessary to restore Gomer and then impose on her the restrictions designed to protect her and to facilitate her purity from that time forward (Hos. 3:3). In like manner, God's unfailing love for Israel precipitated His taking the necessary measures to restore them to Himself (part of the subject of Part 3).

So looking at Hosea's life with Gomer up close and personal pictures something about God's sovereign grace in saving an undeserving people, and also His sustaining grace that remains steadfast regardless of the sins and failures of His covenant people. I have said this before, but it is the conclusion that we cannot miss. From a human perspective, from the beginning Hosea's love for Gomer did not make sense. From a human perspective, Hosea would have been justified in abandoning Gomer to her own lusts and inclinations. But God made Hosea a public man, put his life on display, and by his life pointed to an infinitely higher and nobler love—His love for sinners. From a human perspective, the gospel makes no sense, and herein is its beauty. Gomer gives hope to sinners: where sin abounds, grace abounds much more (Rom. 5:20). Grace, notwithstanding its sovereignty, is not capricious. It is impossible to think about grace without thinking about God's only provision to deal with sin. God's eternal plan to deal with sin has always been to send His Son, the Curse-Reverser, the only Redeemer of God's elect: "so grace might reign through righteousness to eternal life through Jesus Christ our Lord" (Rom. 5:21). Hosea's life pointed to Christ.

The Message of the Children

Although the primary symbolism of Hosea's life flows from his relationship with Gomer, the Lord also assigns symbolic significance to the three children: Jezreel, Lo-Ruhamah, and Lo-Ammi. The symbolism is transparent from the names given at their births. As I have suggested, "children of harlotry" (Hos. 1:2) means that they shared their mother's latent propensity to immorality and consequently added to Hosea's parental worry. However, their function in the prophecy is not to intensify Hosea's grief but to declare God's discipline of His disobedient people.

They all speak of necessary judgment: Jezreel, the irony of it (Hos. 1:4); Lo-Ruhamah and Lo-Ammi, the tragedy of it (Hos. 1:6, 9).

The birth of Jezreel is a portent first of the demise of Jehu's dynasty (752 B.C.) and then of the collapse of the entire northern kingdom (722 B.C.): "Call his name Jezreel, for in a little while I will avenge the bloodshed of Jezreel on the house of Jehu, and bring an end to the kingdom of the house of Israel" (Hos. 1:4). The initial significance of the name *Jezreel* ("God scatters or sows") does not relate to its meaning but to a historical allusion. This statement concerning the house of Jehu is somewhat difficult because it seems to contradict 2 Kings 10:30. In that historical narrative the Lord directly commends Jehu for doing what was right in God's eyes by fulfilling the Lord's heart in the execution of Ahab's house in Jezreel. However, the idea expressed by the translation "I will avenge the bloodshed of Jezreel on the house of Jehu" suggests that now the Lord is punishing Jehu's house for what in the other text brought commendation. The solution to the paradox is in the verb translated "avenge" (*pqd*). This verb can mean nothing more than to inspect or give attention to something. Although when it occurs with the preposition translated "on" (*'al*) it frequently has the sense of "punish," it literally conveys the idea of seeing the direct object (here the blood of Jezreel) to be on the object of the preposition (here the house of Jehu).[19] As Ahab's dynasty ended in bloodshed, so will Jehu's dynasty, but there is no direct blame being put on Jehu. Here, then, is the irony of this judgment: The act of obedience that initiated the dynasty of Jehu will, because of sins as heinous as those associated with Ahab's house, bring the same judgment.

God's necessary discipline for disobedience is a major theme in Hosea's message, and with the symbolic naming of Jezreel the Lord juxtaposes two aspects of the coming judgment. First, He announces the end of Jehu's dynasty, which from its inception was limited to four generations (2 Kings 10:30). When Shallum assassinated Zechariah after six months on the throne, that initial prophecy was fulfilled (2 Kings 15:8–10)—and so was Hosea's prediction regarding Jezreel that the dynasty would end in bloodshed. Second, God announces the fall of the whole northern kingdom (2 Kings 17:6, 23). Hosea's tenure of ministry witnessed the first, and the second was soon and certainly to follow.

The message of the next two children is transparent. *Lo-Ruhamah* means "no mercy," and the Lord forthrightly explains the significance: "For I will no longer have mercy on the house of Israel" (Hos. 1:6). *Lo-Ammi* means "not my people," and the Lord again forthrightly explains: "For you are not My people" (Hos. 1:9). The message of Lo-Ruhamah and Lo-Ammi is as tragic as it is transparent. "No mercy" results in national disaster. "Not my people" reveals what seems to be a reversal of the covenant. God's declaration that Israel is His people and that He is their God is the essence of covenant language (see Ex. 6:7). Although the covenant is ultimately unconditional because of God's saving purpose in Christ, individual participation was always conditioned on or, perhaps better, evidenced by faith in the promise. Hosea's generation had forsaken the Lord and owned no claim to God's promise. Therefore, not only did God disown them, but He punctuated the disclaimer by saying, "I will not be your God" (Hos. 1:9).

Although most versions translate the last line of verse nine this way to correspond to the normal covenant formula, the Hebrew text literally says, "and I myself will not be for you." This could be rendered "even I, I will not be yours," but I tend to see the preposition "for" as expressing advantage rather than possession. Paul asked the question, "If God is for us, who can be against us?" (Rom. 8:31). That is a fair question at any time. The idea obviously is that if God is for us, then none can be against us—at least effectively. The converse is just as true. If God is not for someone, then that person is susceptible to any and all opposition. Israel was going to find out the consequences of God's not being on its side. It was going to fall to foreigners. Judgment was inevitable. Lo-Ammi meant Lo-Ruhamah!

Judgment was coming, but restoration was to follow. Hosea's reunion with Gomer anticipated the restitution, and the names of the children—though not the children themselves—were used to point to the happier future. In Hosea 2:23, the prophet describes the day when the nation will experience God's blessing. Playing on the name *Jezreel*, the Lord says, "Then I will sow her for Myself in the earth." This is not a scattering in judgment but an expansion in blessing, an advancing of the kingdom. Playing on *Lo-Ruhamah*, the Lord says, "I will have mercy on her who had not obtained mercy." Playing on *Lo-Ammi*, the Lord says, "Then I will say to those who were not My people, 'You are My people!' And they shall say, 'You are my God.' " The good news of this curse-reversal applies to more than national Israel. Peter recognized the full gospel implication when he applied this promise to believers of the New Testament dispensation: "But you are a chosen generation, a royal priesthood, a holy nation, His own special people, that you may proclaim the praises of Him who called you out of darkness into His marvelous light; who once were not a people but are now the people of God, who had not obtained mercy but now have obtained mercy" (1 Peter 2:9–10). There is indeed much gospel according to Hosea.

Paul said of the Corinthians that they were "manifestly an epistle of Christ" (2 Cor. 3:3). How well the message of Christ could be read in the Corinthian people is arguable. But the statement is most applicable to Hosea, and the message of the gospel his life declared was written in black and white. It was on the surface for all to see. By his life, he evangelized the people around him. Looking at Hosea and his family up close and personal outlines his message. He lived what he preached, and he preached what he lived.

FOR FURTHER REFLECTION

1. What was unique about Hosea's ministry in comparison to other prophets?
2. In what way does Gomer give hope to sinners?
3. How does your past/present life magnify the grace of God?
4. Think again about how your life should demonstrate the grace of the gospel.

PART THREE

THE SERMON

Not to practice what is preached is hypocritical. To preach what is not first personally practiced is to propagate theory. Hosea was neither a hypocrite nor a theorist. He was genuine, and his message poured from personal experience. What he preached was what he lived. The transparency of his personal life reinforced the credibility of his public preaching. His public preaching was confrontational, boldly direct, and purposeful—always aiming for a verdict. He was—as it were—a "street preacher" taking the Word of the Lord to a sinning people, not a professional theologian reflecting on society's ills at a clean and comfortable distance. Hosea preached against sin—specific sins—declared the devastating consequences of sin, and proclaimed God's gracious acceptance of genuine repentance. In simple terms, Hosea preached the gospel.

Before proceeding, I need to explain why I am calling Part 3 "The Sermon." Obviously, I am using the term loosely. It would be neither accurate nor fair to evaluate Hosea by current methods and standards of homiletics. It would certainly not be exact to envision Hosea standing behind a pulpit addressing a seated congregation after the congregational singing. I do not know the venue in which Hosea would have communicated his message verbally—this message that ultimately under inspiration he wrote into the canon of Scripture. Whether Hosea's message can be legitimately classified as a sermon or not, it is certainly a message from the Lord. What was said of the prophet Haggai years later could well describe Hosea: "The LORD's messenger" who "spoke the LORD's message to the people" (Hag. 1:13). Sermon mechanics can be taught, but the Lord's message must be received. The sermon is just the structured vehicle to communicate the message. What is said takes precedence over how it is said, but that is not to say the structure is not important. Bad structure can obscure the best of messages.

Even though Hosea's message may not fit into any particular homiletical category, it does include elements that every well-structured sermon ought to contain. There is an introduction that grips the attention, establishes the need, and points to the resolution. There is an unequivocal declaration of the Word of the Lord that gives authoritative weight to what is said; it was not just the prophet's opinion. There is an effective incorporation of appropriate and vivid illustrations to elucidate the salient points. There are the requisite general and specific applications to implement truth into life. Ultimately, it is the pointed applications that distinguish a sermon from a lecture. That being said, Hosea preached a sermon.

At this juncture, I want simply and briefly to remark on Hosea's homiletical skill. You may remember that in the first chapter I observed the obvious division of Hosea into two principal sections: the biographical details (Hos. 1–3) and the preaching details (Hos. 4–14). I also noted that there were six hope sections in Hosea that may mark the progression of his argument (Hos. 1:10–2:1; 2:14–23; 3:4–5; 6:1–3; 11:8–11; 14:1–8), and that the charges of no faithfulness, no lovingkindness, and no knowledge of God (Hos. 4:1) may express the logic of his development.

Not only are these possible markers of the book's structure, but they also indicate something of Hosea's homiletical genius. Interestingly, half of the hope sections occur in the first three chapters. These chapters constitute the introduction to the sermon, the message in miniature. Hosea's personal story certainly grabs the attention; Hosea then establishes the need for the message with the stated parallels to Israel's sin; and he anticipates the resolution of the need with the three predictions of restoration, the last of which is unreservedly messianic (3:5). The body of the sermon follows with three main points, all containing sufficient proof of their respective propositions that Israel is without faithfulness, lovingkindness, and knowledge of God, and all ending with a word of hope. There follows a brief and pointed conclusion urging the listeners to understand and implement all that has been said (Hos. 14:9).

An introduction, three points and a conclusion—sounds like a sermon.

CHAPTER SIX

THE GRACIOUS COVENANT

Most of the data in Hosea regarding God's gracious covenant with Israel concerns the nation's betrayal of it and God's determination to bring it to new covenant idealism and realization.[1] The renewal of the covenant with Israel that Hosea predicts both symbolically and directly, however, presupposes its initiation; the covenant had a definite beginning. Depending on one's eschatological schemes, there may be a definite future for the nation Israel as well, but a full discussion of that issue waits another day.[2] The focus on the national covenant—whether past or future—does not distract from the spiritual significance; there are both parallels and straight lines leading directly to the covenant of grace made possible by Jesus Christ and applied irresistibly and infallibly to every regenerated heart. God's dealing with Israel is a paradigm of saving grace. The New Testament recognizes this when it links Moses with Hosea and then applies the gracious statements to individual believers:

> But you are a chosen generation, a royal priesthood, a holy nation, His own special people, that you may proclaim the praises of Him who called you out of darkness into His marvelous light; who once were

> not a people but are now the people of God, who had not obtained mercy but now have obtained mercy. (1 Peter 2:9–10, alluding to Moses in Ex. 19:5–6 and the prophet in Hos. 2:23)

With this New Testament warrant, we have every right and reason to glean from Hosea's sermon to Israel timeless and universally relevant truths about the gospel.

Per the delimitation set in the introduction, this study will offer neither a verse-by-verse commentary nor a section-by-section synopsis of Hosea's prophecy. Helpful resources are available that provide this kind of assistance.[3] Rather, this study will isolate predominant salvific themes along with enough supporting evidence from Hosea to demonstrate that the prophet indeed preached the gospel. The first theme concerns the gracious covenant that initiated the relationship between God and Israel. Seeing the full gospel and christological focus in this covenant emphasis depends on factoring in what we have already considered about the nature and essence of all of God's covenant dealings. That is, at the heart of every revelation of the covenant is God's intent to provide the Curse-Reverser (chapter 3). With the amount of covenant theology antecedent to Hosea, it is not a hermeneutical stretch to see that his use of the concept was intentionally christologically charged.[4] Although there may not be an explicit reference to Messiah in view in every verse or even every chapter, failing to see Christ in what Hosea says about the covenant is to miss what he says. Very simply stated, the message of Christ is inherent in Hosea's covenant theology. Find God's covenant, and you find God's Christ.

What Hosea says about God's making a covenant with Israel (Hos. 2:18) and the nation's subsequent breaking the covenant (Hos. 6:7; 8:1) encapsulates the thoughts of divine grace, displeasure, and faithfulness.

At this point our attention is on God's grace and the manifestations of His sovereign love.

THE INITIATION OF THE COVENANT

Remember that there are two kinds of covenant: suzerainty treaty (monopleuric—between a superior and an inferior) and parity contract (dipleuric—between equals). Any covenant with humanity that God is a part of is invariably monopleuric: God has no equal. God is infinitely superior and absolutely sovereign in every revelation and institution of His covenants. He initiates the contact with those with whom He chooses to enter covenant, sets the terms and obligations of the relationship, and issues the guarantees of blessing contingent upon compliance and of reprisals consequent upon violation. Although many of the suzerainty-type treaty covenants from the ancient Near East exhibit the same components, they were normally generated from military conquest and from the self-serving interests of the superior. A victorious king would impose and enforce his will on a defeated and, most likely, unwilling people. In contrast, God altruistically initiates His covenant with a people made willing by grace—for their good and His glory.

Expressed in Terms of Love

Hosea's development of the covenant in terms of marriage rather than military conquest is, therefore, noteworthy. Regardless of differing marriage customs that are temporally or culturally defined, there is one constant: a marriage is somebody's idea. Somebody makes the first move to initiate the relationship. In the spiritual marriage bond, God is the instigator. When God instructed Hosea regarding his relationship with Gomer, He marked His love for Israel as the standard by which Hosea was to love

Gomer: "Go again, love a woman . . . just like the love of the LORD for the children of Israel" (Hos. 3:1). Why this is a key verse in Hosea should be clear enough. Not only does it explain Hosea's symbolic ordeal, but it lays the foundation for the overriding spiritual message. It is hard enough to grasp the magnitude of Hosea's love for Gomer; God's love is totally beyond comprehension.

It is not surprising that a book about marriage and family should refer so often to love. The root word for love (*'hb*) occurs almost twenty times in Hosea: the common noun *'ahavah* three times (3:1; 9:15; 11:4); the rare noun *'ahavim* once (8:9); the verb *'hb* fifteen times (2:5, 7, 10, 12, 13; 3:1 [three times]; 4:18; 9:1, 10; 10:11; 11:1; 12:8; 14:4). What is surprising is that the majority of occurrences refer to Israel's illicit love associated with their spiritual adultery of pagan worship. This only spotlights the wonder of God's love for them (3:1; 11:1, 4; 14:4)—variously expressed through the imagery of both husband and father—and points to the real issue of love. The marriage/family motif certainly speaks of the natural affection that ought to be the experience of every family. Yet the word for love goes far beyond expressions of affection, no matter how deep-seated those affections may be. This love finds its impetus in the will. It designates a compelling inclination of the heart to a chosen object. At the heart of love—marriage love not excepted—is the exercise of choice. A man may know any number of women, but he chooses one to be his wife, the special object of his love. This does not mean that he abhors all other women or that his choice of bride constitutes unfair treatment of the other women he did not choose. But by selecting one woman to be the object of his special love, he rejects all others. Similarly, at least in our culture, a woman has the prerogative to accept or reject whatever proposals come her way. Prospective husbands, at least in our culture, do not usually pick their brides by drawing straws; there is instead something about their prospective bride that attracts them and generates love.

Permit me a personal reflection to make the point. I vividly remember the first time I saw the woman who has become my wife. Something about her triggered a pitter-patter inside me; something about her was attractive to me. I remember how long it took me to muster the courage to meet her, and once I met her, how quickly I fell in love. That was it. I fell in love—just could not help myself. I found that the more I learned about her, the more I loved her. There was something about loving her that made sense—to me she was lovable. The time came when I made a conscious decision never to love another as I loved her, and I chose her to be my wife to the exclusion of every other woman on the planet. Rather than causing all the other girls on campus to mourn the loss, that decision was reason for celebration by all who knew us. It was a happy day. All of that was over thirty-five years ago, and I have never changed my mind about loving her. It started with an attraction and a pitter-patter, both of which thankfully remain to this day, but there is more to my love for her than emotional affection. Love became choice, and that loving choice made sense.

Here's the point I want to make. God did not fall in love with Israel. From the outset, His love was a matter of choice. He decided to love them, and the reason for that loving choice was not in their attractiveness or worthiness. Moses forthrightly said that, in essence, God loved Israel because He loved them (Deut. 7:7–8). God's love is totally of grace. The motive for God's gracious, electing love is within Himself, not in the objects of His choice. That is what makes grace so amazing. God chose Israel in spite of what they were, not because of what they were. He knew their sin, their weakness, their bent to evil, and their inability to love Him perfectly in return (again note Hosea's delineation of all they loved instead of God). All this fits well with the suggested interpretation of Hosea's marriage to Gomer. Thanks to God's special revelation to Hosea about Gomer, his love for her was not blind. He knew what he was getting. Neither was God's love for Israel blind; He knew what He was getting, and He loved them nonetheless. According to His own testimony, God declares, "I will love them freely" (Hos. 14:4). The word *freely* has the idea of doing something "of one's own accord."[5] Had God not loved Israel of His own accord, He never would have loved them.

As amazing as God's love for Israel was, it was not unique to ancient Israel. It was an object lesson, a paradigm, of His gracious operations. We can easily see in others what is often hard to see and to admit in ourselves, but the way He loved Israel is the way He loves all His elect. Because He is who He is, and because of His infinite and sovereign love, He has chosen us in spite of what we naturally are and in spite of all He knows about us. Even though we are capable of loving Him because He loved us (1 John 4:19), we can never and will never love Him as we ought to love or as He deserves to be loved. He knows it; yet He loved us and loves us still. It betrays a high degree of spiritual insensitivity not to see ourselves in Hosea's Gomer or in God's Israel and not to see the wonder of God's loving us.

Now, then, consider this straight line to Christ. Since marriage is a covenant and since God enters into such a covenant with His chosen people, He does so in terms of Christ, because Christ is at the heart of God's gracious covenant. It is only through Jesus Christ, the Curse-Reverser, that God's love for sinners is knowable or possible to experience: "In this is love, not that we loved God, but that He loved us and sent His Son to be the propitiation for our sins" (1 John 4:10). He demonstrated this love while we were still sinners (Rom. 5:8). Talk about grace!

Remembered in Terms of Redemption

The references to the exodus in Hosea's prophecy are not just incidental details from Israel's diary but rather intentional reminders that God initiated His relationship with Israel and that He did so in covenant terms. The Lord declared, "When Israel was a child, I loved him, and out of Egypt I called My son" (Hos. 11:1), and then He reminded the people twice that He was the Lord their God "ever since the land of Egypt" (Hos. 12:9; 13:4). Hosea's alluding to the historical exodus was a means of reminding Israel that God had redeemed them from slavery in keeping His covenant promise to their ancestral father Abraham and had entered into national covenant with them as Abraham's seed—an epochal point in the progression of redemptive history leading to the gospel's fullness of time in which Abraham's ideal Seed would come. There was no event in Israel's history more important than the exodus. Politically, it marked the birth of a nation; religiously, it pictured the gospel. In the Old Testament, including in Hosea, every reference to the exodus is theologically pregnant, and we miss the point as interpreters if we ignore that theological fullness. The fact that the details are not delineated does not mean that the details are not there. Any mention of this historical event is a theological catalyst to trigger gospel and christological thoughts and a hermeneutical signal to factor those thoughts into every specific context of reference. One reason so many readers of the Old Testament miss so much of the gospel is the failure to recognize theologically loaded terms and to unload them into the interpretive process. Hosea's references to the exodus, therefore, point to essential truths about the gospel that would have been, or at least should have been, known to his congregation. Unloading exodus theology into Hosea's allusions is to uncover something of Hosea's message of Christ.

Resisting the temptation to develop a complete theological analysis of Exodus, I will sum up the salient gospel truths to remember about the exodus when considering Hosea's allusion to the event.[6] First, the exodus is a reminder that *salvation is from sin's bondage*. God delivered the nation from a terrible estate of misery from which they could not free themselves. Egypt held them in an iron furnace of affliction. From birth they were slaves, forced to labor by cruel taskmasters, held under alien domination. Likewise, in the spiritual realm, every man is enslaved to an alien power from which there is no escape and over which there is no control: "whoever commits sin is a slave of sin" (John 8:34). The power of sin is internal as well as external. Israel was in bondage not only to the Egyptians, but also to their own wills and subject to the same guilt as their idolatrous masters. They were not being persecuted for sainthood in Egypt; they were justly being punished for their own iniquity (Josh. 24:14; Ezek. 23:8, 9, 21). Birth in sin's bondage always transitions to sinful behavior. The exodus reminds us of what we were.

Second, the exodus is a reminder that *salvation is because of sovereign grace*. The exodus eve was marked by life and death. Some lived; some died. The question is why. Since the Israelites were as iniquitous and guilty as the Egyptians, the only explanation rests in God's sovereign will: "I will be gracious to whom I will be gracious, and I will have compassion on whom I will have compassion" (Ex. 33:19; see also Rom. 9:15–18). Grace is humbling and unattractive to those who think they have or can earn divine favor, but without it there is no salvation. The exodus reminds us that salvation is all of grace and that damnation is all of merit.

Third, the exodus is a reminder that *salvation is by irresistible means*. This highlights the beauty of the gospel: God does for man what he cannot do for himself. Moses proved earlier that redemption requires more than the arm of flesh. The exodus highlights God's irresistible power, expressed both in word and in deed. References to His strong hand and mighty arm declare the Lord's strength (Ex. 6:1, 6; 13:9; 15:6–9, 11). References to His signs and wonders reveal His strength (Ex. 4:8, 17, 28, 30; 7:3; 8:23; 15:11). The plagues, the hardening of Pharaoh's heart, and the opening of the sea for crossing all demonstrate His power over things that would seem to be beyond control. The exodus also highlights the irresistible power of the blood of sacrifice as the means of redemption. The Passover events climax the whole exodus drama (Ex. 12). Grace, notwithstanding its sovereignty, could not be experienced without atonement. The blood of the lamb, shed and applied, was the difference between life and death. The exodus Passover reminds us that salvation is achieved outside of ourselves by a perfect substitute whose blood is shed for the remission of sins.

Fourth, the exodus is a reminder that *salvation is to great privilege*. Grace never leaves sinners where it finds them; they always experience a transformation. The exodus brought the people into the privilege of sonship (Ex. 4:22–23). They enjoyed a special relationship with God, who brought them into existence, would rear them, would provide for them, would love them, and would chastise them as any father would his son. Hosea directly plays on this in 11:1. The exodus brought the people into the privilege of fellowship; they would become His people, indeed His special treasure (Ex. 5:1; 7:14; 8:1; 19:5). Hosea plays on this motif in the naming of Lo-Ammi, "not my people." The exodus brought the people into the privilege of holiness (Ex. 19:6). They were to enjoy a position of dignity that distinguished them from the world around them; they were set apart to be like their God. So much of Hosea plays on Israel's failure to be a holy people; they resembled the world rather than the Lord. Finally, the exodus brought the people to the privilege of service. They were saved to serve the Lord through their obedience and their worship. Interestingly, the same word that Exodus uses to describe servitude to the Egyptians describes service to the Lord. The former service was harsh and cruel; the later service pleasant. The master makes all the difference. So the exodus reminds us that God's grace has made us special, and that should be a motivation to holiness in life.

That is exodus theology in a nutshell. It does not require a great deal of spiritual acumen to see the parallels to the gospel and the straight lines drawn directly to Christ. It is not surprising that the allusions to the exodus flow deep in both the Old and the New Testaments. What God did then because of His covenant and compassion and by means of His infinite power and vicarious atonement had significant and relevant meaning for Hosea hundreds of years after the fact, and it has the same meaning for us thousands of years later. God's covenant grace is everlasting; His power never diminishes; and His purpose to pass over those under the blood is eternally certain.

I have taken the time and space to open this nutshell because the purpose of our study is to discover what Hosea says about the gospel generally and Christ specifically. Admittedly, I have said far more about the exodus than Hosea said. Although Hosea does not explicitly detail the events of the exodus, his allusions to that monumental event served as catalysts for thought. Hosea's seemingly passing remarks about the exodus event were calculated to jog the nation's memory of what God had done at the beginning of their national existence to set forth Christ evidently before them, for that is exactly what He did in the ceremonial rituals He revealed consequent to their leaving Egypt. Mentioning the exodus would be like our referring to July 4, 9/11, or June 5 (my wedding anniversary); and, most parallel for the Christian, it would be like mentioning Calvary. The simple references conjure up big pictures. To remember the exodus was to remember all the attendant circumstances of plagues, of Passover, of safe passage through the sea, and of covenant ratification at the foot of Sinai, where the nation then freely pledged their allegiance and vowed their obedience to the Lord. For Hosea's nation to remember the exodus was incentive to their admission of guilt and motive for repentance. Bringing up the exodus was good preaching. The exodus was more than history: its message is the everlasting gospel.

THE EXPRESSIONS OF THE COVENANT

When God enters into covenant, He gives ample evidence that a covenant does in fact exist. Blessings and benefits are always in attendance. Hosea's message draws attention to some of those evidences[7] to magnify the heinous character of Israel's violation of the covenant terms. Israel's disobedience of the covenant was smack in the face of indisputable evidence of all the good God had done for them.

Intangible Expressions

Sometimes the intangible expressions of love and relationship are the most intimate and meaningful. Husbands and wives often use endearing names for each other, some known only to themselves as exclusive expressions of their mutual affection and singular bond. Some, like "honey" or "sweetheart," are generic, lacking originality but nonetheless effective when uttered between husband and wife. Others are unique, reflecting thoughtful imagination, like the one I use for my wife and which will go with us to the grave. But whether common or individual, those terms of endearment are intangible expressions of an intimate relationship and are, therefore, special.

Now here is my point. The name or descriptive expressions by which God refers to Himself communicate important information: the designation sends a message. The names of God, in fact, are essential components of God's Self-revelation in the Scripture, particularly in the Old Testament. Each reveals something about His person, His perfections, or His work. The names and titles of God never occur haphazardly or merely according to the personal preference of an individual author. The significance of each must be factored into the interpretation of the whole context in which the name occurs. In these appellations, God graciously condescends to our necessarily finite way of thinking. God is without limit in all of His attributes simultaneously, but we can think about only one thing at a time. Each Self-revelation limits our thoughts about Him to one or another of His perfections or works. So, for instance, *El Shaddai* (God Almighty) draws attention to His all-sufficiency and power, *El Elyon* (the Most High God) to His majesty, *El Olam* (the Everlasting God) to His eternity, *Adonai* (Lord) to His sovereignty, and so on.

The way Hosea refers to God in his prophecy is, therefore, an important component of his overall message. While it would be inappropriate to speak of any of God's names as endearing, it is significant that the principal designations of God in the prophecy do draw attention to the special relationship that exists between God and His people: they are expressions of the covenant.

The name *Jehovah* or *Yahweh* (LORD) occurs forty-six times in the book, appearing in every chapter.[8] *Jehovah* is the unique proper name of the one true and living God; in a wonderful sense it avers God's absolute independence, self-existence, and infinity—the fullness of His august person.[9] But in addition to what it reveals about His essential being, the name *Yahweh* is the special covenant name of God closely associated with His interest in, salvation of, and faithfulness to His people.[10] That this is Hosea's predominant designation of God throughout his prophecy reinforces the prominence and importance of the covenant theme. It intimates the personal nature of the relationship between God and the nation, highlighting the magnitude of His grace to them and of their affront against Him. He revealed His most special name as evidence of His love, and they spurned Him. It was all very personal.

Also significant is Hosea's use of the general word for deity usually translated "God" (*'elohim*). Whereas *Yahweh* refers to God's immanence, *'elohim* typically points to God's creating power and inherent majesty. It occurs twenty-two times in every chapter except ten and eleven. But the significance is that in eighteen of those twenty-two occurrences, Hosea connects the title to a personal possessive pronoun (my God, your God, her God, their God).[11] This combination effectively emphasizes the intimacy of God's gracious relationship with His people. Although as God He is so infinitely higher than the creature, He graciously condescends to bind Himself personally with His covenant people. It is, in fact, a key expression in covenant declarations that the covenant people will especially belong to Him and He to them: "I will be their God, and they shall be My people" (for instance, Ezek. 37:27).

How the prophet refers to God expresses much about divine grace. The designations are intentional and calculated, on the one hand, to convey the message of covenant grace and, on the other hand, to put in bold the very personal nature of Israel's covenant violations. In a very real sense, David's confession appropriately applies to the nation's transgressions as well: "Against You, You only, have I sinned" (Ps. 51:4). These two ways of referring to God may well be intangible evidences of His love and gracious covenant, but they are precious evidences nonetheless.

Since we are on Christ-alert in our study of Hosea, we should not miss the direct connection the divine name *Jehovah* has to Jesus, even beyond the meaning of His name, "Jehovah saves." *Jehovah* is the name owned by each of the persons of the Trinity. The Scripture very directly connects the name to Jesus Christ. John's gospel, particularly, makes the identification. For instance, the apostle refers to Isaiah's famous vision and says, "These things Isaiah said when he saw His glory and spoke of Him" (John 12:41). Unmistakably John is speaking of Christ, which is momentous in the light of Isaiah's identification of whom he saw: "For my eyes have seen the King, the LORD of hosts" (Isa. 6:5). In another place, during a confrontation with unbelieving Jews, Christ said that their father Abraham rejoiced to see His day. This led to a most significant exchange. The Jews said, "You are not yet fifty years old, and have You seen Abraham?" (John 8:57). Christ's answer astounded them and intensified their anger: "I say to you, before Abraham was, I AM" (John 8:58). The "I AM" is an unmistakable application to Himself of the name *Jehovah*, the unique covenant name of the one true and living God. One thing is for sure. Notwithstanding the Jews' hatred of Jesus, they well understood the implications of His theology. Certainly, if unbelieving Jews got the point, so should we.

Another intangible expression of God's covenant relationship with Israel is His communication with them. Relationships thrive on communication, and they wither without it. The health of any family depends on open communication: without it, husbands and wives drift apart, and parents and children frustrate each other. It was one of the special benefits of God's election of Israel that they became the vehicle through which God revealed His Word and His redemptive purpose ultimately leading to Jesus Christ. The apostle Paul remarked on this truth: "who are Israelites, to whom pertain the adoption, the glory, the covenants, the giving of the law, the service of God, and the promises; of whom are the fathers and from whom, according to the flesh, Christ came, who is over all, the eternally blessed God. Amen" (Rom. 9:4–5). In the ultimate sense, God's giving His Word to and through Israel was the means of His grace to us all, but historically in the course of redemption, it was a singular demonstration of His covenant love for Israel.

It is not surprising, then, that Hosea's focus on the covenant relationship in terms of husband/wife as well as parent/child would include references to God's special communication to His bride/son. In Hosea 8:12, the Lord declared, "I have written for him the great things of My law." The word *law* (*torah*), the most general designation in the Old Testament for special revelation, encompasses all of God's Word, not just legislation or commandments. Although the immediate reference here may well be the legislation at Sinai (see Deut. 4:6–8), other statements in Hosea indicate that the divine revelation was not limited to that one auspicious occasion. In reviewing all of God's past dealings with the nation, Hosea reminded the people that it was "by a prophet the LORD brought Israel out of Egypt, and by a prophet he was preserved" (Hos. 12:13). The Lord Himself said, "I have also spoken by the prophets, and have multiplied visions; I have given symbols through the witness of the prophets" (Hos. 12:10). The significance of this, of course, is that prophets stood in God's place as His mouthpiece to the people. The prophet's speaking was God's speaking.

Through this speaking to His people, the Lord made it clear both what He was like and what He liked—that is, what would please Him. Interestingly, one of the chief accusations leveled against Israel was their lack of knowledge about God (Hos. 4:1), which led to every conceivable sin (Hos. 4:2). The implication is that had they known Him, they would have avoided those sins. There is something about knowing God that produces behavior that is pleasing to Him. Their ignorance of God was not because God did not make Himself known, but rather because they did not listen. To know God is to fear Him; to fear God is to love Him; to love God is to keep His commandments. So God's giving His law was ultimately a means of aiding His people to love Him. It was a gracious thing for Him to do. In many ways, one's response to God's law is an index to one's response to God's grace. If there has been a work of grace in the heart, there is a desire to please the Lord. The Lord in His kind wisdom has not left His people guessing as to what pleases Him: He gave His law.

Let me offer this illustration. My wife and I have two sons. I believe these boys have always loved me and have genuinely wanted to please me. When they were growing up, I did not want them to wonder about what would please me and to become frustrated as they tried this and that. Because I loved them, I established in our home what we called "Barrett-law." They knew that so long as they lived within the sphere of "Barrett-law," I would be pleased—no guessing. Obeying these rules was not the condition for becoming a Barrett but the evidence of the family name they owned by birth. Barretts lived a certain way. Life was good when they lived within that circle, and there were consequences when they got outside the lines. The purpose of "Barrett-law" was not to make life miserable for them but to instruct them as to how they should live as a Barrett. My pleasure continues as I see them grown with families of their own, establishing "Barrett-law" for the next generation.

Significantly, God did not give Moses the law at the burning bush as a condition for delivering the nation from bondage. He delivered them graciously. At Sinai, He gave the law to a people already redeemed, who had graciously been declared to be His son, His firstborn. The great things of God's law defined how God's children were supposed to live—no guessing. The law and every other word that God spoke were expressions of His love. Israel's disobedience to God's law was a rejection, therefore, of His love.

It is imperative to remember—whether in the Old Testament or in the New—that the law is a servant of grace and the gospel, never their enemy. For sinners, the law sets an unattainable standard of righteousness that convicts of sin and points to Christ, whose vicarious obedience of the law earned the necessary righteousness and perfection required for acceptance with God. As Paul says, the law is the "tutor to bring us to Christ" (Gal. 3:24). The gospel does not replace the law but rather fulfills it in Jesus Christ. In Christ, believers are free from the law as a means of earning life, merit, and favor with God. In Christ, believers are free from the penalty and condemnation of the broken law. In Christ, believers have the freedom, ability, and desire to obey the law as a way of life that pleases God: the law defines the borders of holiness. The law is full of gospel. Hosea's references to the great things of the law and the constant prophetic witness to God's communication were just one more way he declared the gospel.

Tangible Expressions

Although the intangible expressions of love and covenant relationship may arguably be the most significant, every so often something touchable is in order. My wife knows that I love her and have vowed before God to be with her for life. However, if on our anniversary I simply announced, "I love you; I'm still here," she might be a little disappointed. Even if it is something small, something goes a long way. Sight reinforces faith. The same holds true in the spiritual sphere. We are to walk by faith rather than sight, but the Lord does not leave His people without tokens of blessings. After all, the Scripture does say, "The LORD will give grace and glory; no good thing will He withhold from those who walk uprightly" (Ps. 84:11). And then again it says, "Every good gift and every perfect gift is from above, and comes down from the Father of lights, with whom there is no variation or shadow of turning" (James 1:17). The Lord provides for His people as evidence of His gracious love.

When God entered the covenant with Abraham, He promised that He would give to him and his descendants "all the land of Canaan, as an everlasting possession" (Gen. 17:8). In Deuteronomy—Moses' great exposition on the covenant and the basis of Hosea's creed—that land is viewed as God's gift to the nation approximately twenty-five times (for examples, Deut. 1:20, 25; 2:29; 3:20; 4:40; 5:16 and more). Deuteronomy 8:7–9 is a classic summation:

> For the LORD your God is bringing you into a good land, a land of brooks of water, of fountains and springs, that flow out of valleys and hills; a land of wheat and barley, of vines and fig trees and pomegranates, a land of olive oil and honey; a land in which you will eat bread without scarcity, in which you will lack nothing; a land whose stones are iron and out of whose hills you can dig copper. When you have eaten and are full, then you shall bless the LORD your God for the good land which He has given you.

God's gift to His people was good, and it was vitally connected to His covenant promise, a promise first made with Abraham and then renewed with Abraham's seed.

Israel's living in the Promised Land should have been a reminder of all that the Lord had done. It certainly fits well Hosea's prevalent use of the family analogy that the Lord as the Husband/Father would supply a home for His family. The tragedy of Hosea's Israel is that they had become so spiritually calloused and blind to the goodness and love of the Lord that they could be right in the middle of all the promised blessing and not recognize it as His gift to them. In fact, they had God's gift in hand and credited their illicit paramours for the bounty: "I will go after my lovers, who give me my bread and my water, my wool and my linen, my oil and my drink. . . . These are my rewards that my lovers have given me" (Hos. 2:5, 12).

You can almost sense the pathos in the Lord's lament, "For she did not know that I gave her grain, new wine, and oil, and multiplied her silver and gold" (Hos. 2:8). A principal part of Hosea's message will be what the Lord will do to prove to Israel once again that He is the giver of every good gift. The land was God's gift, but enjoying the gift was contingent upon faith and obedience to stipulations of the covenant.

Remember as well that this land theology draws yet another line directly to Christ. A key idea of dwelling in the land was the experience of rest, and that physical rest was symbolic of a greater spiritual rest. As we learned in considering Hosea's creed, to be in the place of rest spiritually was to experience the presence and fellowship of God. That symbolic rest typifies the ultimate rest that is found solely in Jesus Christ. You can see justification for this typical significance in Hebrews 4:4–11, an overview of the theological progression of rest climaxing in the rest accomplished by Jesus Christ: creation rest, Sabbath rest, Canaan rest, eternal rest, and redemptive rest. Thus, Christ graciously extends the invitation to come to Him in order to receive the rest He gives (Matt. 11:28), and Hebrews admonishes, "Let us therefore be diligent to enter that rest" (Heb. 4:11). What a gift that rest is. The connection may be subtle, but the gift of the land touches the gospel.

The remarkable note about Hosea's theology of covenant grace is not so much the volume of references but the weight of what seem to be incidental statements. It is important, therefore, not to pass over the theologically infused buzzwords and allusions. This consideration of God's gracious covenant in Hosea has not covered many verses in the prophecy, but it has reflected on a foundational truth that relates to everything else the prophet says. The covenant is the essence of Hosea's good news, his gospel message.

FOR FURTHER REFLECTION

1. Can you think of any good reason God should love you?
2. What points of similarity can you see between what God did at the exodus and what He has done in saving you?
3. How is the law an expression of grace?

CHAPTER SEVEN

THE BROKEN COVENANT: THE BRIGHT SIDE

In one sense, this chapter is going to be a digression, at least regarding the specifics of Hosea's prophecy. It is, however, a necessary excursion designed to keep Hosea's contribution to the gospel in the proper perspective, particularly in the context of all his details about Israel's sin.

Just as Gomer betrayed Hosea, broke her covenant of marriage, and committed adultery, so Israel acted treacherously against the Lord by breaking the covenant and committing spiritual fornication. Most of Hosea's prophecy exposes and delineates Israel's sin in no uncertain terms. Admittedly at first glance, there appears to be very little gospel—good news—in most of what Hosea has to say in his sermon. But appearance and reality very often are not the same. Israel broke God's gracious covenant, and that was tragic. Yet as heinous as their sin was against God, it was an integral and connected component in the development of God's ultimate purpose in redemption. Nothing frustrates grace. Strangely yet wonderfully, there is a bright side to Israel's breaking the covenant.

Although Hosea points to and predicts the redemptive goal achieved by Israel's breaking the covenant, the apostle

Paul provides an inspired and authoritative theological analysis of the whole matter of Israel's rejection of and by God and its place in God's redemptive agenda (Rom. 9–11). Were it not for Paul's explanation, we might miss something of the magnitude of Hosea's message, but even with it there remain some significant questions. Since the focus of this study is Hosea's contribution to gospel revelation, we will necessarily survey his exposé of Israel's specific sins against the covenant. However, the fact that Paul quotes Hosea 1:10 and 2:23 in his authoritative exposition indicates that Hosea made some contribution to the big picture of redemptive history and warrants our apparent digression beside the point. Looking first at how Israel's sin fits in the scheme of redemptive history reveals the bright side and will help put the dark side in gospel perspective. In this regard, I want to reflect briefly on two questions raised by Israel's breaking the covenant: how it could happen and why it happened.

HOW

The first question is how. Contrary to expectation, Israel spurned God's love. Logically, it does not make any sense that a people so favored and loved by God would or could treat the Lord as they did. Normally, love answers love; as the apostle averred, "We love Him because He first loved us" (1 John 4:19). That is what should be expected: loving God in response to His love is the logical and sensible thing to do. Sin, however, perverts everything, including the mind's ability to think correctly. Sin is folly, and Hosea recognizes the foolishness of Israel's behavior when he describes Ephraim as "a silly dove, without sense" (Hos. 7:11). On the one hand, how Israel could so treat the Lord in view of His loving kindnesses to them is illogical indeed. But that is sin, the only explanation.

On the other hand, the more perplexing question is theological. If God chose Israel to be His special people, His bride, and entered into covenant with them, how could they reject Him as they did? This is particularly puzzling to us Calvinists who believe in the irresistibility and irreversibility of grace, especially when we consider God's saving acts toward Israel as paradigmatic and typical of His saving acts for all His elect.[1] Answering this question has two parts: defining the nature and extent of the covenant with ancient Israel and determining the identity of Israel. These are huge concerns that go beyond the actual data of Hosea but are foundational to understanding Hosea's place in redemptive history. Keeping within the scope of this study prohibits a thorough consideration of all the issues and implications, so I can only cover a few key matters.

The Nature and Extent of the Covenant

Aspects of God's covenant with Israel were corporate and external. Although this covenant with the physical descendants of Abraham was full of gospel revelation, as a temporal administration of the covenant of grace, it was, nonetheless, a national covenant[2]—the bylaws governing social and political as well as religious behavior. Regardless of the profoundly vivid gospel truths portrayed by Israel's being delivered from Egypt's harsh bondage, that deliverance was not equivalent to being delivered from sin's bondage. Being within the national covenant was conditioned by physical birth, not spiritual birth. Spiritual salvation has always depended on regeneration, not generation. This was the main point of Christ's evening lecture to Nicodemus regarding the necessity of the new birth (John 3:1–21). That this necessity is not just New Testament theology is evident from Christ's question revealing His astonishment at Nicodemus's ignorance: "Are you the teacher of Israel, and do not know these things?" (John 3:10).

Although a national covenant, it nonetheless communicated the message of grace and was the means of bringing the elect of God into the full experience of His saving and covenant grace. Yet the possibility of being within the national covenant without spiritual salvation is a frequent concern in the Old Testament. This is evident, for instance, in how both Moses and the prophets viewed circumcision, the visible sign of covenant membership. It is striking that Moses, in addressing the uncircumcised generation of Israel about to enter the Promised Land, says nothing about circumcising the flesh. He does, however, implore them to circumcise the foreskin of the heart, a great symbol of regeneration (Deut. 10:16). Similarly, Jeremiah, in addressing a people who were circumcised in the flesh, issued the same instruction for them to circumcise the heart (Jer. 4:4). All of this sounds very Pauline: "For he is not a Jew who is one outwardly, nor is that circumcision which is outward in the flesh; but he is a Jew who is one inwardly, and circumcision is that of the heart, in the Spirit, and not in the letter" (Rom. 2:28–29).

Salvation is personal, yet in the progress of revelation God worked with Israel on a corporate level to put on view important lessons with relevance to the individual. The covenant that constituted Israel as a nation did not necessarily extend to the hearts of every Israelite, but the covenant of grace revealed in that specific temporal covenant did extend to the hearts of some. The elect were saved in terms of the covenant of grace and consequently kept faithfully all the demands of the temporal covenant. But because unregenerate sinners also populated the nation, the covenant was breakable.

This is the difference between the terms of the essentially national covenant and the essentially spiritual new covenant. One is breakable; the other is not. This seems to be at the heart of what Jeremiah says about the new covenant. Unlike the covenant at Sinai that marked the birth of a nation, the new covenant is individual, internal, irresistible, and irreversible:

> Behold, the days are coming, says the Lord, when I will make a new covenant with the house of Israel and with the house of Judah—not according to the covenant that I made with their fathers in the day that I took them by the hand to bring them out of the land of Egypt, My covenant which they broke, though I was a husband to them, says the Lord. But this is the covenant that I will make with the house of Israel after those days, says the Lord: I will put My law in their minds, and write it on their hearts; and I will be their God, and they shall be My people. (Jer. 31:31–33)

It is important to understand that the essential components of what Jeremiah terms the new covenant were and are present in every temporal administration of the covenant of grace. This is why the New Testament speaks of salvation in the language of the new covenant (Heb. 8:7–13). Salvation through grace has always operated the same way. The salvific revelation included in Israel's national covenant underscores the power of sin to blind the sinner's eyes to grace. It was possible to be an Israeli citizen and thus be in middle of gospel grace and truth, and yet reject grace and break all the terms of the covenant. Grace is not irresistible until and unless God embeds it in the heart.

So back to our question: how could Israel break the covenant? The answer is tragically simple. The nature and extent of the temporal administration of the covenant are one part of the answer: some aspects of the covenant were only external. The nation was filled with sinners, who, although partakers of visible and external blessings and recipients of gracious revelation, stood accountable for the privileges but remained outside the realm of saving grace. Individual participation in the covenant of grace was founded in God's election and conditioned by faith and obedience. Without that divine election and its consequent regeneration, sinners remain oblivious to even the most obvious spiritual truths. Jeremiah puts it this way when describing the cursed man who departs from the Lord: "he shall be like a shrub in the desert, and shall not see when good comes" (Jer. 17:6).

The Identity of Israel

The consequence of the co-existence of external and internal aspects of the covenant with Israel was a spiritually divided nation: the nation was an admixture of God's elect and the non-elect. The apostle Paul acknowledged this admixture when he declared, "For they are not all Israel who are of Israel" (Rom. 9:6). Significantly, he dates the dichotomy antecedent to the birth of the nation by stating further, "nor are they all children because they are the seed of Abraham. . . . That is, those who are the children of the flesh, these are not the children of God" (Rom. 9:7–8). Christ stated the same. In one of His exchanges with the Jews of His day, the Lord Jesus granted, on the one hand, that they were Abraham's descendants (John 8:37) and then, on the other hand, denied that they were Abraham's children, identifying their father as the devil (John 8:39–40, 44). In simple terms, there is a national Israel, and there is a spiritual Israel. Spiritual Israel is a subset of physical Israel, sometimes designated as the remnant (e.g., Isa. 1:9).

Yet ultimately, "spiritual Israel" is more inclusive than the visible nation. Israel, in this spiritual sense, becomes one of the labels for God's elect regardless of nationality. Thus, for example, Paul refers to the Gentile-based Galatian church as "the Israel of God" (Gal. 6:16). In fact, he sets aside ethnicity, social status, and gender, declaring all believers to be "one in Christ Jesus" and part of "Abraham's seed" (Gal. 3:28–29). It is integral to covenant soteriology that there is one body of God's elect from every age: "The catholic or universal Church, which is invisible, consists of the whole number of the elect, that have been, are, or shall be gathered into one, under Christ the Head thereof; and is the spouse, the body, the fullness of Him that filleth all in all" (Westminster Confession of Faith, 25.1). "Israel" or "Abraham's seed" are ways of referring to that spiritual body.

All of this bears on our question as to how Israel could have broken the covenant. The answer partly depends on which Israel is in view—spiritual or physical. In one sense, both were always present because there was always a remnant according to the election of grace (Rom. 11:5), similar to the visible church, which includes both the wheat and the tares. In the Old Testament, sometimes the political entity seems to be at the fore and at other times the spiritual; discerning which one is being referred to complicates the interpretation process. Suffice it to say that it was the nation as a visible whole (with its substantial constituency of unbelievers) that broke covenant with God, and God dealt with the visible nation accordingly. In spite of the presence or preserving power of the spiritual remnant (Isa. 1:9), in the terms of the national covenant God dealt with the body as a whole. There was hegemony in the corporation sometimes beneficial to those undeserving and other times detrimental to those not guilty. But the simple fact that not all Israel is Israel explains how Israel could break the covenant.

WHY

Answering the question why it happened unveils the bright side of Israel's transgression; it highlights God's unfailing purpose and plan of redemption. The course of redemption does not always develop according to expectation, but it does progress without deviation. God does not adjust His plan in reaction to what may appear to be obstacles; on the contrary, God is in such total control of time and circumstance that He factors opposition into His plan as a means of revealing His glory. Whether we can comprehend it or not, God used Israel's sin as a means of achieving His worldwide redemptive purpose.

This is where Paul's theological analysis in Romans 9–11 particularly contributes to our understanding. Paul shows that Israel's rejection did not signal any failure of God's Word. On the contrary, he systematically proved by logic and Old Testament evidence that God would infallibly save all the elect, that Israel's rejection of gospel grace was partial and temporary, and that it was designed to turn the gospel to the Gentiles. That is the bottom line and the bright side: Israel's rejection was the means of bringing the gospel to the Gentile world. Israel's transgression translates to our salvation. Paul says forthrightly, "through their fall . . . salvation has come to the Gentiles" (Rom. 11:11). Significantly, the apostle cites Hosea as evidence of God's intent to include Gentiles in His covenant:

> "I will call them My people,
>   who were not My people,
> And her beloved,
>   who was not beloved.
> And it shall come to pass in the place
>   where it was said to them,
> 'You are not My people,'
> There they will be called sons
>   of the living God" (Rom. 9:25–26, quoting
>   Hos. 2:23; 1:10).

If that is what the inspired Paul said Hosea meant by that prophecy, then that is precisely what the inspired Hosea meant. In other words, even Hosea, while experiencing the dark side of Israel's sin, saw the light. His exposing Israel's sin was part of His gospel message.

One of the most remarkable things to me is how, in the course of redemptive history, God over and over uses the wrath of men to praise Him and to advance His eternal agenda. Follow the line of redemption, and you cannot miss seeing this truth. The first announcement of the covenant of grace came immediately after sin entered the world, and the Lord announced to what was then the entirety of the human race that a Curse-Reverser would come. Sin led to grace. But it seemed that sin would frustrate grace as wickedness spread rampantly throughout the world, earning God's judgment in the flood destruction. Grace, however, prevailed and preserved the human race through Noah and his family. The sparing of humanity preserved redemption's plan. Nevertheless, as the human race multiplied, so did sin, and the events of Babel again seemed to jeopardize the promise. But sin and judgment led to grace in the election of Abraham and the narrowing of the promise to his descendents. Yet the promise of worldwide blessing remained intact, and the question was how it would get back on track. God used Israel's sin as the means. It was the world's sin that narrowed the gospel promise to Israel; ironically, it was Israel's sin that widened the gospel again to the world.

That is the big picture, and it helps to put the specifics in focus. God's using Israel's sin as a means of accomplishing His purpose of grace does not excuse or justify that sin. The Lord held them accountable and dealt with them justly in the light of all the privileges they enjoyed. Sin always has consequences, but it does not frustrate grace. Keeping the bright side of Israel's transgression in view does not diminish the dark side of sin, but it does magnify the beauty, power, and irresistibility of God's redeeming grace.

FOR FURTHER REFLECTION

1. What is the potential danger of going to church?
2. Think of instances where God has used people's sins to accomplish His own glory and good for His people.

CHAPTER EIGHT

THE BROKEN COVENANT: THE DARK SIDE

Sin does not frustrate grace; rather, sin is the occasion for grace to shine. In the providence of God, Israel's breach of covenant advanced the gospel: it marked a critical moment in God's redemptive plan to save a people from every race, nationality, and place on earth. God is sovereignly capable of turning man's wrath to the praise of His glorious grace. God's sovereignty, however, neither conflicts with nor circumvents human responsibility. The darkness of sin does not eclipse the brightness of grace; nor does the brightness of grace diminish the darkness of sin. In stark contrast, then, to the bright side of Israel's sin that expanded the covenant to worldwide application and enjoyment was a dark side that was heinous and ugly. There is nothing good about sin, not even when God makes use of it to achieve His glory.

Israel's response to God's love should have been humble gratitude, devotion, and loving obedience, but it was not. They overstepped the bounds of the covenant terms and behaved treacherously against the Lord. What magnifies the ugliness of Israel's sin is that it occurred in spite of such enormous privilege. No nation on earth has ever experienced what Israel experienced. Moses summed it up well:

> For ask now concerning the days that are past, which were before you, since the day that God created man on the earth, and ask from one end of heaven to the other, whether any great thing like this has happened, or anything like this has been heard. Did any people ever hear the voice of God speaking out of the midst of the fire, as you have heard, and live? Or did God ever try to go and take for Himself a nation from the midst of another nation, by trials, by signs, by wonders, by war, by a mighty hand and an outstretched arm, and by great terrors, according to all that the LORD your God did for you in Egypt before your eyes? To you it was shown, that you might know that the LORD Himself is God; there is none other besides Him. Out of heaven He let you hear His voice, that He might instruct you; on earth He showed you His great fire, and you heard His words out of the midst of the fire. (Deut. 4:32–36)

What Moses said about Israel's uniqueness in comparison to all the nations preceding them applies equally to all those since then. There never has been another nation—before or after—that enjoyed such special privilege: "For what great nation is there that has God so near to it, as the LORD our God is to us . . . ?" (Deut. 4:7). With great privilege come great responsibility and increased accountability: "For everyone to whom much is given, from him much will be required" (Luke 12:48). Israel sinned in great light. How dark was that?

As a gospel preacher, Hosea spoke to the sin issue head-on. Preaching the gospel always entails preaching against sin, warning of sin's consequences, and announcing sin's remedy. Hosea did it all. In terms of volume, the greater part of Hosea's message addressed the details of Israel's breach of covenant. Israel sowed to the wind, and they would certainly reap the whirlwind (Hos. 8:7) because God was holy and just. Hosea uncovers the dirty details of Israel's sin not only to mark the contrast with God's holiness and justice but also to put in bold His constant faithfulness to His covenant promises. Although spurned, God's love remains constant. That sums up the theme of Hosea's sermon. In order to put Hosea's good news in perspective, an overview of his bad news is necessary.

THE ESSENCE OF ISRAEL'S SIN

The short version of Israel's sin is that it was a breach of covenant. The Lord summarized the reason for the nation's impending judgment in these terms: "Because they have transgressed My covenant . . ." (Hos. 8:1). Similarly, in Hosea 6:7, the Lord says about Israel, "But like men they transgressed the covenant. . . ." Whether *'adam* (men) in this verse refers to humanity generally or to Adam specifically has significant theological implications beyond the context, but in the immediate context the essence of the accusation is clear: the nation overstepped or passed over (*'br*, transgress, in both 6:7 and 8:1) the borders set by the covenant agreement. In light of how we have defined and must understand the essence of the covenant, this was no small matter. To transgress the covenant was tantamount to rejecting the gospel—to rejecting Christ.

At the root of this breaking of covenant was the plain fact that the nation lived in willful oblivion to God: they forgot the Lord (Hos. 8:14; 13:6). In fact, Hosea 13:4–6 tracks the very progression of degeneration that Moses had warned about centuries earlier: from exodus redemption to wilderness dependence to prosperity in the land to forgetfulness.

> Beware that you do not forget the LORD your God by not keeping His commandments, His judgments, and His statutes which I command you today, lest . . . when your heart is lifted up, and you forget the LORD your God who brought you out of the land of Egypt, from the house of bondage; who led you through that great and terrible wilderness . . . then you say in your heart, 'My power and the might of my hand have gained me this wealth.' And you shall remember the LORD your God, for it is He who gives you power to get wealth, that He may establish His covenant which He swore to your fathers, as it is this day. Then it shall be, if you by any means forget the LORD your God, and follow other gods, and serve them and worship them, I testify against you this day that you shall surely perish. (Deut. 8:11–19)

Grasping the full force of this root sin depends on understanding the implication of forgetting (*shkkh*) and remembering (*zkr*) in the Old Testament. Normally in our way of thinking, we have little control over what we remember and what we forget. Perhaps it betrays my advancing age, but there are things I forget that would be to my advantage to remember. Conversely, seemingly insignificant things pop into my mind from years ago, some of which I would like to forget. Sometimes we try our best to remember things only to forget them; other times we long to forget only to remember.

Without doubt, the ancient Israelites suffered from this same involuntary mental malady, but the Hebrew words involve much more than uncontrolled mental reflexes. Remembering and forgetting are volitional terms: they are acts of the will. To remember is consciously and willfully to think about something. To forget is consciously and willfully to refuse to think about something. Forgetting God, therefore, is a most serious offense. The psalmist said, "The wicked shall be turned into hell, and all the nations that forget God" (Ps. 9:17). If that divine sentence applies to every nation who refuses to think about God, how much more does it apply to Israel whose special relationship with the Lord gave them so much more to think about (see Amos 3:2)! In the face of national election, covenant revelation, and redemption, Israel acted without reference to God, thus breaking the covenant. They forgot Him on purpose.

Hosea sums up the essence of Israel's sin in terms of forgetting God and breaking the covenant; he delineates the parts of the sum in his initial summons to the nation to "hear the word of the LORD" (Hos. 4:1). Using courtroom jargon, Hosea declares that the Lord is bringing charges against the inhabitants of the land and then specifies three broad accusations: no truth, no mercy, and no knowledge of God. Significantly, the center charge of no mercy hits at the heart of covenant violation, and its being framed by the absence of truth and ignorance of God explains its nonexistence. Not only do these three indictments expose the dark side of breaking the covenant in general terms, but in reverse order[1] they set the main points of Hosea's sermon in which Hosea presents irrefutable proof of the charges (see the suggested outline in Chapter 1). It is not pretty.

No Truth

In evidence of this first charge, the last section of Hosea's prophecy (Hos. 11:12–14:9), which by and large proves the accusation of no truth, begins with a specific and blunt statement of the nation's deception: "Ephraim has encompassed Me with lies, and the house of Israel with deceit" (Hos. 11:12). In one sense, the charge of no truth is broad enough to encompass the whole indictment. The word *truth* (*'emeth*) is a general term whose base idea is firmness, dependability, or trustworthiness. The absence of truth in the land, therefore, includes the notions of

Israel's unreliability and untrustworthiness with reference to the stipulations of the covenant. In simple terms, they could not be counted on to keep their word or meet their obligations; they could not be trusted. Consequently, the nonexistence of truth in the land (untrustworthiness) resulted in mendacity in both word and deed. When the foundation of truth is abandoned, there is no standard for practicing truth—anything goes. Rather than standing on the firm foundation of God's truth, the nation fed on the wind, pursued the east wind, and not surprisingly, increased lies daily (Hos. 12:1). They lied to God—"My God, we know You" (Hos. 8:2; see also 7:13; 11:12); they lied to others—"Deceitful scales are in his hand" (Hos. 12:7); they lied to themselves—"They shall find in me no iniquity that is sin" (Hos. 12:8).

No Mercy

The charge of no mercy is the center accusation and comes to the very heart of the covenant relationship. It is something God desired more than religious ritual (Hos. 6:6), so its absence is solemn. The word *mercy* (*khesedh*) is a covenant buzzword designating the loyalty of attitude and behavior mutually required from and rightfully expected by the parties in covenant with one another.[2] *Khesedh* is a covenant obligation; it is based on and flows from a relationship. It connotes both love and love's appropriate action, whatever that action may be. Here is an illustration that may clarify the point. If I saw a woman stranded with a flat tire, I might stop and change the tire. That would be a kind gesture expressing compassion and pity. However, if I were on a tight schedule or in my work clothes (coat and tie) I could pass by, feeling duly sorry for her but feeling no obligation to help. If, on the other hand, that woman were my wife, regardless of schedule or attire or anything, I would stop, change the tire, or at least call our roadside assistance number and wait with her for help to come. The relationship demands my action in her behalf. That is *khesedh*.

Here is the point. By covenant God has obligated Himself to His people to do for them whatever is appropriate. His covenant mercy—His loyalty—never fails. It is, in fact, a theme of frequent praise. The repeated refrain of Psalm 136 says it well: "For His mercy endures forever."

Israel owed the same consistent loyalty to the Lord, a loyalty that could be expressed only by their faithful obedience to the covenant stipulations. But contrary to expectation, their loyalty was temporary and unsubstantial. The imagery of Hosea 6:4 describing Israel's covenant loyalty is too vivid to misunderstand: "For your faithfulness [*khesedh*] is like a morning cloud, and like the early dew it goes away." Now you see it; now you don't. The way of thinking and the way of behaving that were most basic to the covenant relationship were tragically missing. This is a serious charge.

No Knowledge of God

Since the word *knowledge* entails both intellectual and experimental aspects, the final charge of no knowledge of God (*da'ath 'elohim*) includes both the lack of apprehension of the truth about God and the nonexistence of any personal experience or relationship with God.[3] Hosea 5:4 stated explicitly, "They do not know the LORD." This lack of knowledge could not be traced to a lack of information. God had revealed Himself and His word in the clearest of language: "And you shall know no God but Me; for there is no savior besides Me" (Hos. 13:4), and "I have written for him the great things of My law" (Hos. 8:12). The many references to Israel's breaking the law—the reflection of God's character—and their perverted preference for Baal testify to their total and willful ignorance of God. The consequence of this spiritual ignorance is severe: "My people are destroyed for lack of knowledge." In the spiritual sphere, ignorance of God and His law is never an excuse; rather, it is reason for condemnation.

Like the accusation of no truth or reliability, this charge of spiritual ignorance is broad enough to account for all the specific sins of which Israel was guilty. Like mercy, knowing God is something the Lord desired more than outward ceremonies (Hos. 6:6) and is the goal of His covenant engagements (Hos. 2:20)—His gospel revelation. The Lord Jesus justifies this gospel link when He brings knowing God to its ultimate implication in terms of spiritual life and death: "And this is eternal life, that they may know You, the only true God, and Jesus Christ whom You have sent" (John 17:3). If not knowing God was the problem, knowing God would be the solution. It is not surprising, then, that Hosea included in his admonitions to repentance the pursuit of the knowledge of God (Hos. 6:3)—a knowledge that necessarily included Christ.

Hosea did not mince words: the essence of Israel's sin was dark, deadly, and comprehensive. But his message is equally clear that where sin abounds, grace abounds more. More about this later.

THE EVIDENCE OF ISRAEL'S SIN

For Hosea, sin was more than theological theory. Sin touched his life—personally, politically, socially, and religiously. As a scorned husband, Hosea experienced firsthand the awfulness of sin in his own home. As a prophet representing God, Hosea would have been equally sensitive to the horror of the sins of his homeland. After all, he understood that what happened between him and his wife was a picture of the even more tragic affront of his nation against his God. The evidence of Gomer's violation of her marriage covenant with Hosea was irrefutable; she was guilty. Likewise, the evidence of Israel's violation of their covenant with God was beyond excuse or defense; they were guilty as charged.

Immediately after Hosea pronounced the Lord's threefold indictment against the nation, he presented the evidence of the nation's guilt in the general terms of the Ten Commandments: "By swearing and lying, killing and stealing and committing adultery, they break all restraint . . ." (Hos. 4:2). Although the entire code is not listed, the entire code is in view since the law is a single unit. Transgression of any one part constitutes guilt against the whole (see James 2:10). But even if that principle were not operative, the specific expressions of Israel's sin that Hosea places into evidence prove that their guilt before God is comprehensive.[4] Socially, they were guilty of all sorts of moral debauchery: violence (Hos. 1:4; 6:8–9); theft (Hos. 6:9; 7:1); fraud (Hos. 7:1, 3; 10:4, 13; 12:1, 7); fornication (Hos. 4:13, 18; 7:4); and drunkenness (Hos. 7:5). Politically, they were guilty of unlawful and ungodly alliances, which reflected their ignorance of God's law and their lack of trust in Him (Hos. 5:13; 7:8, 13, 16; 8:4, 9–10; 12:1). But far and away, Hosea gives evidence of Israel's religious sins. These religious crimes address the heart of covenant violation and account for all the other sins as well. Transgressing the first great commandment requiring total devotion to the Lord makes it impossible to obey the corollary commandment of loving one's neighbor.

Hosea's sermon in many ways provides a casebook of sin. Most of the standard Old Testament words for sin are scattered throughout the prophecy in addition to others that are specifically suited to Hosea's particular focus on the breach of covenant. For instance, the word most often translated as "sin" (the root *kht'*) occurs in either verb or noun form at least eleven times (Hos. 4:7, 8; 8:11 [twice],13; 9:9; 10:8, 9; 12:8; 13:2, 12). This is the word that provides the image many of us have heard since our Sunday school days of missing a target. It vividly pictures sin as the failure to conform to the standard of God's righteous and inflexible law. The noun usually translated "iniquity" (*'awon*) occurs at least as frequently (Hos. 4:8; 5:5; 7:1; 8:13; 9:7, 9; 10:13; 12:8; 13:12; 14:1, 2). This word pictures sin as twisted, perverted, or deviant behavior. Significantly, this is the principal word in the Old Testament to designate the guilt of sin, and sometimes—although rarely—even the punishment of sin. Thus, when this word occurs, the interpreter must determine whether the text is referring to the actual sin or the guilt that results from the sin. Another commonly used word for sin usually translated as "evil" or "wickedness" (*ra'*) occurs eight times (Hos. 7:1, 2, 3, 15; 9:15 [twice]; 10:15 [twice]). This word pictures sin as disastrous or calamitous behavior: sin is destructive. Other key words, such as "to rebel" (*psh'*), occur less frequently (Hos. 7:13; 8:1; 14:9); some contextually specific words, such as "to play the harlot" (*znh*) and "to commit adultery" (*n'p*), occur more frequently (Hos. 1:2 [twice]; 2:2, 4, 5; 4:12 [twice]; 5:3, 4; 6:10; 9:1 and Hos. 2:2; 3:1; 4:2, 13, 14; 7:4 respectively). But all are instructive, whether picturing sin as corruption (*shakhath* in Hos. 9:9); reproach (*kherpah* in Hos. 12:14); shameful behavior (*bwsh* in Hos. 2:5); lewdness (*navluth* in Hos. 2:10); deceit (*'awen* in Hos. 6:8; 10:8; 12:12); or stubbornness (*srr* in Hos. 9:15).

Even as isolated terms in a vocabulary list, these and all the other words Hosea uses to refer to Israel's covenant violations underscore the heinous character of sin. The fact of the matter is, however, that no theology is ultimately defined by individual and isolated words, and these words do not occur as mere lexical entries. Truth is stated by proposition, and Hosea's propositions regarding sin only add to the darkness. Since such a predominant proportion of Hosea's message is taken up with declarations and descriptions of sin in order to prove the charges leveled against Israel, an analysis of his sin-theology could almost take the form of verse-by-verse commentary. Each of the three principal divisions of Hosea's sermon (4:1–6:3;

6:4–11:11; 11:12–14:9) discloses something of the corruption of Israel's sin, the consequent condemnation that the sin earns, and the gracious call to repent from the sin. Avoiding the temptation to comment on this development sequentially, I want to summarize Israel's religious sin since it represents the fundamental expression of their breach of covenant.

Hosea's congregation presents a clinical case of empty religion. They were full of religion but without any spiritual profit: "With their flocks and herds they shall go to seek the LORD, but they will not find Him; He has withdrawn Himself from them" (Hos. 5:6). Given the condition of their heart, their religious ritual was the last thing God wanted: "For I desire mercy and not sacrifice, and the knowledge of God more than burnt offerings" (Hos. 6:6). When religion takes shape without the knowledge of God, it will invariably miss the mark of what is acceptable to God and profitable to the soul. During Hosea's day, there were three main religions in practice in Israel. Each distinguished itself from the others by its object of and approach to worship: the right God in the right way, the right God in the wrong way, and the wrong god in every way. Hosea himself was a member of the remnant church who worshipped the one true and living God in the way He prescribed. It was Hosea's mission to see converts to the true religion. His mission field included those who followed the state religion instituted by Jeroboam I—in name worshipping the right God but in a way contrary to His prescription—and those who abandoned the Lord totally in exchange for Baal.

Although the official state religion and the renegade worship of Baal may have looked different in particulars and practice, Hosea did not differentiate regarding the degree of deviance. He summed up any departure from the one true way of worship as dealing treacherously against the Lord (Hos. 5:7; 6:7). This verb *bgd* sometimes refers to the unfaithful violation of a marriage bond and thus aptly describes Israel's faithless breaking of the covenant. Jeremiah 3:20, for instance, directly links these two spheres of violation: "Surely, as a wife treacherously departs from her husband, so have you dealt treacherously with Me, O house of Israel, says the LORD." Significantly, the first statement the Lord makes regarding Israel's breach of covenant uses the imagery of fornication: "the land has committed great harlotry by departing from the LORD" (Hos. 1:2). Not only is the image graphic, but the language is emphatically certain.[5] Hosea reiterates this charge over and again to stress the heinous debauchery of Israel's breaking their special relationship with the Lord: "For the spirit of harlotry has caused them to stray, and they have played the harlot against their God" (Hos. 4:12; see all the other references listed above for both *znh* and *n'p*). Given the visual aid of Gomer's betrayal and Hosea's heartbreak, the gravity of Israel's offense is not hard to understand. God demands and deserves total devotion from His people. Such blatant disregard of the Lord in abandoning Him for other gods while throwing a few worship trinkets His way was an insult to His character and His goodness. It was harlotry at its worst.

This spiritual adultery showed itself in three significant ways. First, the nation switched their religious devotion from the Lord to Baal. Hosea 2 boldly draws the line from Gomer's adultery to Israel's. The Lord accuses the nation of playing the harlot, going after other lovers, and forgetting about Him (Hos. 2:5, 13). He identified the illicit lover as Baal (Hos. 2:8, 17), whom Israel credited with providing sustenance that in reality came from the Lord (Hos. 2:5, 8, 12). Baal (*ba'al*) is not so much a proper name of a god as it is a descriptive title, meaning "master," which designated an imagined god to be the head over other imagined gods. It was a title commonly used among Israel's neighbors to honor whomever among a plethora of gods they regarded as supreme. There was a commonality in Baal mythology throughout the region, although the specific identity of the designated Baal would differ from place to place: Hadad, Dagon, Chemosh, etc. It was essentially a fertility cult involving various rigmaroles of rituals—often lewd ones—possibly to insure the productivity of the land in each agricultural cycle. It was a religion for profit—worshipping in order to procure stuff for living. Whom Israel regarded as their Baal is not specified; neither is it relevant. What is significant is that under the influence of their pagan neighbors and out of selfish motives, they worshipped a god of their own conception.

Second, the nation abandoned true, spiritual worship for sight worship: they committed idolatry. According to Hosea 4:12, idolatry is a definite consequence of the nation's spiritual fornication: "My people ask counsel from their wooden idols, and their staff informs them. For the spirit of harlotry has caused them to stray, and they have played the harlot against their God." Similarly, the tragic statement of Hosea 4:17–18 connects idolatry with its expressions of perverted worship to harlotry: "Ephraim is joined to idols, let him alone. Their drink [offering] is rebellion, they commit harlotry continually." Furthermore, Hosea explicitly links Israel's Baal worship to idolatry: "But when he offended in Baal, he died. Now they sin more and more, and have made for themselves molded images, idols of their silver, according to their skill; all of it is the work of craftsmen" (Hos. 13:1–2). That God regards idolatry of any sort or fashion as an abomination and a personal insult is obvious from the most cursory of Bible reading. Paul's assessment of Gentile guilt is just as appropriate for Israel, who suppressed the truth God had revealed to them, traded it for a lie, and "changed the glory of the incorruptible God into an image made like corruptible man" (Rom. 1:18, 23, 25). Idolatry facilitates worship since it is always easier to operate by sight than by faith, but it is dark and serious sin.

Third, they tried to pacify the Lord with increased rituals. It is as though in their religious ignorance and pagan-like superstition they were trying to cover all the bases, giving to every deity they heard of what they thought would make that deity happy and earn them some relief. But they were certainly not giving the true God what He wanted. God was not impressed with their efforts. Listen to Hosea's assessment of their worship. "Ephraim has made many altars," but the Lord said it was for sin: "They have become for him altars for sinning" (Hos. 8:11). The Lord further said, "For the sacrifices of My offerings they sacrifice flesh and eat it, [b]ut the Lord does not accept them" (Hos. 8:13). With a touch of holy sarcasm, Bethel—"house of God," and a center for Israelite worship—was called Beth Aven—"the house of iniquity" (Hos. 4:15; 5:8; 10:5, 8). Sacrifices had to be offered from a proper heart relationship to God. Ritual without a heart alive to God is absolutely meaningless; external religion is nothing unless the heart is right. For Israel to assume that God would accept their sacrifices was just one more piece of evidence proving their ignorance of God.

Heartless worship is always offensive to God. Tragically, the notion seems to be deeply ingrained in man that formal acts of worship—whatever form they take—constitute legitimate worship that will by its very performance be accepted by God. People tend to form their opinions of God from their estimations of themselves. Because they satisfy themselves with outward acts of ritual, they assume that God must be satisfied as well. Many today without Christ assume that going to church and keeping the golden rule will somehow accrue to their favor in the end. Even many who profess Christ allow their pious religious routines to substitute for private devotion and a sincere heart. To estimate God in this way is either to question His omniscience—that He is able to see the heart—or His moral perfection—that He cares about the heart. In contrast to all this human reasoning is the divine preference for heart obedience over manual religion: "Behold, to obey is better than sacrifice" (1 Sam. 15:22).

The bottom line is that in so many ways and contrary to so many spiritual benefits, Israel was unfaithful to the Lord. Their spiritual adultery with all of its attendant shame expressed itself in depravity in every area of life: the nation rejected God's Word (Hos. 8:12; 11:2) and turned away from Him (Hos. 11:7). Very simply, they spurned God's love.

FOR FURTHER REFLECTION

1. Why is it important for preachers to address the issues of sin?
2. What does it mean to remember the Lord? What are some good memory aids to use so as not to forget Him?
3. In Hosea's day, some people professed to worship the true God but in the wrong way, and others worshipped false gods. Can you identify the same religious sins today?

CHAPTER NINE

THE WAY BACK HOME

There's no place like home. Allurements to wanderlust with illusions of greener pastures or greater experiences elsewhere often dim the attraction of home, but after all is said and seen, that fact remains: there's no place like home. Often it takes the hard lessons of the road and distant places to stir up fond memories of home and better times. The grass is not always greener nor the experiences greater, after all. Yet sometimes the wanderings have led so far from home that returning seems impossible. The Lord's story of the prodigal and wayward son in Luke 15 vividly illustrates a kind of tragedy that has been repeated many times. Notwithstanding the comforts of home, discontent and a desire to experience the world took him far away, and he sowed his proverbial oats. But it was not long before the sowing/reaping principle kicked in (Gal. 6:7–8; Hos. 8:7), and he found himself in destitution and despair. At the end of the road, having reached the bitter end of his rope, he remembered home, swallowed his pride, and humbly returned. Happily, his father was waiting for him with open arms; the door to home was still open. That story had a happy ending and points to wonderful spiritual truths.

In many ways, Hosea's personal life with Gomer and his public ministry with Israel parallel the steps of the prodigal in Christ's story. Gomer had a good life with Hosea, but she strayed far from home. Israel enjoyed special status and privilege as God's chosen nation but left the Lord for the ways of the world. Both had wandered so far away that returning seemed unlikely, if not impossible. But just like the father in Christ's story, Hosea took Gomer back (Hos. 3:1–3), and God was ready to take Israel back as well in spite of how far they had wandered. The Lord lamented, "My people are bent on backsliding from Me," but nonetheless He rhetorically asked, "How can I give you up, Ephraim?" (Hos. 11:7, 8). The door to home was still open.

Irrespective of whatever eschatological implications may attend God's offer of hope to Israel, God's strategy for restoring the wayward nation highlights wonderful truths about the gospel that are timelessly relevant. When the Lord took His eternal notion to save a people, His grace was set to find them and save them no matter how far any particular one of them may stray. The Lord does what must be done to bring His elect to Himself. There is no reason to despair of grace; it is amazing. There is encouragement also for saints who for whatever reason fall victim to spiritual wanderlust: there is a way back home. In light of this part of Hosea's message, I cannot help thinking of the verse of the old hymn that ought to be the confession and prayer of every Christian:

> O to grace how great a debtor
> Daily I'm constrained to be!
> Let Thy goodness like a fetter
> Bind my wand'ring heart to Thee.
> Prone to wander, Lord, I feel it,
> Prone to leave the God I love;
> Here's my heart, O take and seal it,
> Seal it for Thy courts above.

Hosea's message of hope is the most beautiful part of his book, and it has earned him the title "Prophet of Love," the St. John of the Old Testament. Hosea's love for Gomer was coerced by divine command but nonetheless existent (Hos. 3:1). If my identification of the "lover" in Hosea 3:1 as Hosea is correct, then his love for Gomer was amazing from the start and remained constant in the face of all his hurt and disappointments. But Hosea's personal expressions of unfailing love paled in comparison to God's love and covenant faithfulness. In fact, it is His covenant love and loyalty that maintained the relationship that was so tragically spurned by sin. This divine love, however, is not impetuous; on the contrary, it is based in eternal reason without violating any aspect of God's righteous being. The Lord's announcement of the renewed marriage covenant with Israel after their wandering is significant: "I will betroth you to Me forever; yes, I will betroth you to Me in righteousness and justice, in lovingkindness and mercy; I will betroth you to Me in faithfulness, and you shall know the LORD" (Hos. 2:19–20). Right in the middle is lovingkindness (*khesedh*). It is God's covenant loyalty or lovingkindness that resolves the apparent tension between divine righteousness and justice with their demands for perfection and God's compassion and faithfulness displayed to those incapable of meeting the demands. There is hope for those prone to wander because the lovingkindness of God endures forever (Ps. 136).

We have already noted how much of Hosea's message concerns the details of Israel's breach of covenant. In connection with Hosea's exposé of Israel's sin is his explanation of how God righteously and justly answers their sin with a view to showing them even more mercy. Interestingly, Hosea 2—the initial application of the Hosea/Gomer analogy to the God/Israel reality—outlines God's plan of restoration for His wayward people: it is the whole book in miniature. After describing Israel's sin in terms of harlotry and adultery (Hos. 2:2–5), God uses three "therefore" statements (*lakhen*) to chart the waypoints on His map for the wanderer to come home: isolation (Hos. 2:6–8); impoverishment (Hos. 2:9–13); and enticement (Hos. 2:14–15).[1] The Lord used each of these steps to highlight the beauty of home. I want to summarize Hosea's overall message of hope under three heads, and along the way we will see the significance of the Lord's isolation, impoverishment, and enticement of His people.

THE OPEN DOOR

Hosea 2:15 suggests the idea of the open door: the valley of Achor—a symbol of judgment since the day of Achan's execution after his sin at Jericho (Josh. 7:26)—was to become a door of hope. Judgment would give way to restoration. Although the open door designates the desired destination, I want to start here because it represents the prospect of hope and thus puts the rest of the message in perspective. Israel had forsaken the Lord: "Woe to them, for they have fled from Me" (Hos. 7:13). As a wife, the nation committed adultery against the Lord, leaving Him for other gods (Hos. 4:17–18; etc.). As a child, the nation rebelled against the Lord's authority, running away from home to find freedom (Hos. 11:1–4). It appeared that Israel had gone so far that returning was not an option. But grace reaches as far as God's intent, and His covenant purposes cannot fail. Hosea's message of hope echoes David's prayer: "For You, Lord, are good, and ready to forgive, and abundant in mercy [*khesedh*] to all those who call upon You" (Ps. 86:5).

The Prospect of Hope

We have already observed that Hosea marks the movements of his message with six distinct sections setting forth the prospect of hope, the open door (Hos. 1:10–2:1;

2:14–23; 3:4–5; 6:1–3; 11:8–11; 14:1–8). Significantly, virtually every one of these messages announcing the possibility of unmerited blessing and restoration follows denunciations of the nation because of their sin and declarations of their merited judgment. The first hint that God was leaving the door open plays on the symbolism of the three named children. Immediately after connecting the children's names to God's judgment of the nation, the prophet declares God's intent and promise to reverse the conditions of that judgment. This first promise is broad, and it encompasses all the specific blessings awaiting the nation when they return home to where they belong. God's scattering the nation (the significance of Jezreel) was set against the prospect of God's gathering Israel and Judah together (Hos. 1:11). God's withdrawing His mercy (the significance of Lo-Ruhamah) was with a view to God's declaring His mercy again (Hos. 2:1). God's disowning His people (the significance of Lo-Ammi) was reversed by His announcement that once again He would call them "My people" (Hos. 2:1).

We'll think about some of the details of restoration in a moment, but first, I want to highlight the simple beauty of the prospect itself. Hosea's judgment/hope cycle exemplifies one of the great "buts" of God's grace. Hosea's logic reminds me of Paul's contrast between spiritual death and life as well as his his resolution of what appears to be a hopeless condition with his hopeful statement, "But God." Having described what it is like to be dead in trespasses and sins (Eph. 2:1–3), he proclaimed the good news, the gospel: "But God, who is rich in mercy, because of His great love with which He loved us, even when we were dead in trespasses, made us alive together with Christ (by grace you have been saved)" (Eph. 2:4–5). Were it not for these "buts" of grace, there would not be salvation for any. If Israel were left alone to pursue the course set by their own will, Hosea's message would be without hope. But there is a message of hope because God intervened in such a way as not to let the nation alone.

The same truth applies to every individual Christian. Had God left us alone to follow our own inclinations, we would remain forever dead and doomed. But God did not leave us alone; He graciously interfered in our hearts, doing what had to be done to bring us to Himself. The interference of grace saved us. That is something to keep consistently in our thoughts; we ought to stay overwhelmed with the reality of grace. Hosea's setting a message of hope before wayward and wicked Israel ought to give hope to sinners that God's grace can reach them regardless of how far from God they are. Hosea makes it clear that God is full of grace—for salvation, for restoration, for preservation. I've said it before, but if Hosea is clear about anything, it is that sinners and wayward saints need never despair of God's grace. This is a truth particularly relevant for Christians who for whatever reasons have strayed from the Lord and then convinced themselves that there is no way back. Hosea says that there is a way back. What a prospect of hope!

The Blessings of Hope

Not only did the Lord leave the door open in prospect of hope, but He allowed the nation a peek inside to see what they were missing and what it would be like when they returned home. Home was an attractive place. Giving them a glimpse of the attractions was a movement of grace to entice them to cease their wanderings and to return. Three particulars of blessing stand out: reconciliation, expansion, and prosperity.

First, a reversal of attitudes between God and Israel suggests the thought of reconciliation. Alienation and hostility would be replaced with relationship and harmony. On God's part, this reconciliation is expressed in His declaration that "not My people" would become "My people" (Hos. 2:23). This is covenant terminology and must be understood in the context of that covenant grace. In terms of the new [renewed] covenant, this transition involves the transcribing of God's law on the heart and includes the forgiveness of sins (Jer. 31:33–34). Without that divine and gracious forgiveness, the sin-caused separation from God would be without resolution (see Isa. 59:2). But it is unique to the one true and living God that He is a God who forgives sins (Mark 2:7; Isa. 43:25). This forgiveness removes the obstacle to fellowship. Hosea records the Lord's own gracious declaration of this forgiveness (using the imagery of healing—see the synonymous parallelism of Psalm 103:3) and attendant consequence of the reversal of His wrath: "I will heal their backsliding, I will love them freely, [f]or My anger has turned away from him" (Hos. 14:4).

God's forgiveness of sin, however, is not impulsive. Forgiveness depends on sacrifice, for "without shedding of blood there is no remission" (Heb. 9:22). Significantly, Hebrews makes this statement in comparing all the animal sacrifices of the old dispensation—so integral to Mosaic theology and worship and therefore to Hosea's—to the infinitely superior sacrifice of the Lord Jesus who shed His blood "once for all, having obtained eternal redemption" (Heb. 9:12). I must emphasize, then, that Hosea did not set forth the prospect of forgiveness in a theological vacuum. We must remember to factor into his message all the antecedent revelation and theology that were so foundational to Hosea's creed. His offer of the blessed prospect of forgiveness assumed the application of the atonement of Christ to which the animal sacrifices of his day pointed.[2] His message of God's reconciling forgiveness was the gospel.

Not only did the blessed hope of reconciliation involve God's reversal of attitude about the people, but it resulted in the people's change of heart regarding the Lord.

Remember that an element of the renewed covenant was the writing of God's law on the heart. When that law is inside, perspectives change; everything looks different, including the Lord Himself. When the law remained outside, the people regarded it as strange (Hos. 8:12), a harsh imposition against their freedom. But the power of grace and forgiveness changes everything. Hosea described the coming change of attitude in terms of the marriage motif: "And it shall be, in that day, says the LORD, that you will call Me 'My Husband,' and no longer call Me 'My Master' " (Hos. 2:16). The blessing of a happy home was right behind the open door.

The beauty and relevance of Hosea's message of reconciliation should not escape us Christians. At the least, this hopeful message should remind us "who once were alienated and enemies" (Col. 1:21) of what God has done for us in Christ: "For it pleased the Father that in Him all the fullness should dwell, and by Him to reconcile all things to Himself . . . having made peace through the blood of His cross" (Col. 1:19–20). Even more we should consider it in the light of Peter's inspired understanding and declaration that Hosea's message of hope applies to us directly, not just by extension. Peter describes the elect (1 Peter 1:2) as those called out of darkness to marvelous light and those "who once were not a people but are now the people of God, who had not obtained mercy but now have obtained mercy" (1 Peter 2:9–10). His congregation was different from Hosea's, but his message was Hosea's message.

Second, home was going to be big. The expansion of the nation was a component of the blessed hope. Interestingly, increase was the first promise in the first hope section (Hos. 1:10–2:1). Immediately after assigning the symbolic significance to the children's names, the Lord announced one of the "buts" of His grace: "Yet the number of the children of Israel shall be as the sand of the sea, which cannot be measured or numbered" (Hos.

1:10). Playing on the significance of Jezreel, He repeated the promise when He said, "Then I will sow her for Myself in the earth" (Hos. 2:23). This increase is yet another of God's provisions in His gracious covenant. Changing the uncountable from sand to stars, God made the same promise to Abraham: "Look now toward the heaven, and count the stars if you are able to number them. And He said to him, 'So shall your descendants be'" (Gen. 15:5). God's promise and intent had not changed in all the hundreds of years between Abraham and Hosea, regardless of how many times and in how many ways the promise seemed to be in jeopardy through unbelief and sin. God's purpose is unfailing, and grace triumphs over sin. That is a blessed hope.

Regardless of the implications this promise may have for national Israel, the main application and significance are to those spiritual descendants of Abraham, believers in Jesus Christ (Rom. 4:16).[3] The church of Christ is eternally determined to succeed; His kingdom will advance. John's apocalyptic vision of the one hundred and forty-four thousand of Israel that were sealed for salvation are specifically identified as "a great multitude which no one could number, of all nations, tribes, peoples, and tongues" (Rev. 7:4, 9). The gospel wins. The full extent of what Hosea prophesied may be even greater than the prophet himself would have anticipated. But it is spiritually exciting to realize that we are a part of the fulfillment and that the fullness of the blessing is still ahead.

Third, prosperity was behind the open door. God's grace is sufficient for every need, and His provision for His people is abundant. Home was an attractive place—no wants, no worries. Hosea measured the prosperity of the restored people in agricultural terms, which in that culture and environment would have been well understood. The Lord would cause the heavens to send to the earth what was necessary to produce grain, new wine, and oil (Hos.

2:22). Hosea 6:3 specifically describes the blessing as God's coming "like the rain, like the latter and former rain to the earth." Hosea 14:5–8 details the benefits resulting from God's dew-like provision, which is evidence of His favor (Prov. 19:12): growth like a lily, stability like a deep-rooted cedar, attractiveness in appearance and aroma like the cedar and olive trees, and fruitfulness. The images are clear enough that life is good at home.

To put all of this in Paul's words, God gives His people "richly all things to enjoy" (1 Tim. 6:17); He lavishes on His people the riches of His grace (Eph. 1:7–8). Paul makes it clear, as well, that the experience of all these spiritual blessings is to be found and enjoyed in Christ (Eph. 1:3). This is not just New Testament revelation either. Solomon, years before Hosea, in a royal and messianic psalm spoke of the Christ-king coming "down like rain upon mown grass, like showers that water the earth" (Ps. 72:6). I would suggest that Hosea had the same topic in mind when he used the imagery of rain coming down to bless. This ultimately and always is the bottom line. The only way man ever has or ever will experience God's blessing and favor is in Jesus Christ. This truth brings us to the next and final thought about the open door to blessing.

The Embodiment of Hope

The apostle Paul stated regarding the Lord Jesus Christ that "all the promises of God in Him are Yes, and in Him Amen" (2 Cor. 1:20). That declaration applied equally to all the promises in the Old Testament and certainly to Hosea's promises of hope to wayward Israel. The Lord Jesus straightforwardly declared, "I am the way, the truth, and the life. No one comes to the Father except through Me" (John 14:6). This dogmatically exclusive declaration did not become true at the incarnation; it was the truth declared first when humanity first needed a message of hope. The seed of the woman was declared to be the coming Curse-Reverser (Gen. 3:15), and every salvific promise that followed advanced the certain coming of the only Redeemer of God's elect. I have stressed throughout this study that Hosea's creed, particularly his covenant theology, rested on the gospel of Christ. Although explicit messianic assertions are minimal, the message of Christ permeates Hosea's theology and must not be overlooked. We are expected to factor in his confession of faith when interpreting the details of his message.

This is not to say, however, that there are no explicit messianic statements. Significantly, direct references to the Messiah occur in some of the hope sections.[4] This is not surprising, since there has never been any prospect of hope apart from Christ. Hosea 1:11 looks to that time when the divided kingdom again becomes a united monarchy under the leadership of "one head." That "one head" must be the Messiah King.[5] Hosea 3:5 says that "the children of Israel shall return, seek the LORD their God and David their king, and fear the LORD in His goodness in the latter days." The relevant statement here is "the LORD their God and David their king." This refers not to a reincarnation of the long-dead king but rather to the incarnation of the LORD their God, the Ideal David—the ultimate fulfillment of God's promise to David (2 Sam. 7:12–16), David's greatest Son. I would suggest translating the "and" as "even" to highlight this identification: "the LORD their God, even David their king." This translation not only identifies the Messiah as the object of seeking faith but also suggests the fundamental truth that the Christ is the God/Man. Hosea's designation of the Messiah as David was not unique. Years later, the prophets Jeremiah and Ezekiel referred to the coming Christ the same way (see Jer. 30:9; Ezek. 34:23–24).

These statements suggest important truths about Christ's nature and mediatorial kingship, but the point for now is simply that Christ is the embodiment of hope. To be without Christ is to be without God, without hope

(Eph. 2:12). Israel's future depended on their encounter and relationship with Christ, just as their ancestral history proved. Hosea reminded his generation of the incident that marked the transformation of their ancestor Jacob and resulted in his new name, Israel (Hos. 12:3–4; Gen. 32:24–28). Jacob recognized that he had a face-to-face encounter with God as he wrestled with the unidentified man. Hosea specifically refers to his combatant as the Angel, a reference to the Angel of the Lord, one of the most significant christophanies in the Old Testament era. A christophany was a pre-incarnate appearance of the Son of God.[6] The message is clear. An encounter with Christ changes life; indeed, it changes everything. It always has, and it always will.

I think you can see why I say that Christ is the embodiment of hope; He is in fact the open door of hope to God. Significantly, Christ identified Himself in those terms. Again, in most exclusive language He said, "I am the door" (John 10:9), the only way to life. He was the only hope in Hosea's day; He remains the only hope in ours.

TOUGH LOVE

I suppose all of us can remember at least one occasion from our childhood when our parents, as they were about to let loose with some discipline, assured us that it was going to hurt them more than it would us. It was hard to believe that then, but my guess is that those of us who have since become parents have used the same line. Maybe our parents were sincere after all—just as we know we are when we say it. Love sometimes requires what is not pleasant for the welfare of those we love. According to Scripture, this discipline, although unpleasant all around, is evidence of love: "He who spares his rod hates his son, [b]ut he who loves him disciplines him promptly" (Prov. 13:24). We usually call this "tough love," but it is love nonetheless.

When Hosea brought Gomer home after her adulteries, he placed her under some restrictions: "You shall stay with me many days; you shall not play the harlot, nor shall you have a man . . . " (Hos. 3:3). In his love for her, he took away some of her freedom, but it was for her good. Similarly, God lovingly brought some hard things upon Israel with a view to their good. His purpose in discipline was to bring the wanderer back where he belonged. The Lord declared that He would do the hard thing of withdrawing Himself from His people to awaken their senses to their spiritual need of Him. "I will return again to My place till they acknowledge their offense. Then they will seek My face; in their affliction they will diligently seek Me" (Hos. 5:15). The means was tough, but the end was good.

I've already suggested that Hosea 2 outlines God's general plan of dealing with His disobedient people, each step with corrective purpose. God would isolate them so that they would recognize His superiority and return to Him (Hos. 2:6–8); He would impoverish them in order to jog their memory of Him and teach them to depend utterly on Him (Hos. 2:9–13); and then once He had their attention He would irresistibly entice them to a renewed relationship so that they would really know Him (Hos. 2:14–20). Much of Hosea's sermon details how God would implement His remedial chastening.

What the nation was to experience could have been avoided by their obedience. The simple fact of the matter is that punishment is earned by disobedience. When my boys were growing up, there were many occasions when I had to enforce some discipline but never once because they obeyed. They knew that disobedience had consequences that they could easily steer clear of if they simply followed the rules. The threat of discipline often was a motive for obedience. Similarly, God had made it clear from the beginning of His relationship with Israel what the rules were and what the consequences of breaking the rules would be. The threat of divine discipline was to be a motive for obedience. Moses clearly made that link for them: "So you should know in your heart that as a man chastens his son, so the LORD your God chastens you. Therefore you shall keep the commandments of the LORD your God, to walk in His ways and to fear Him" (Deut. 8:5–6).

Remember from our earlier discussion of Hosea's creed (Chapter 3) how foundational Mosaic theology was to everything the prophet preached. In so many ways, Hosea mirrors Moses. The threat of imminent discipline that Hosea announced corresponded to the upfront warnings that Moses forthrightly set before his generation (particularly in Deut. 11, 28, and Lev. 26). Barrenness (Hos. 2:2–13), drought (Hos. 4:3), defeat (Hos. 10:14), destruction (Hos. 5:9), and dispersion (Hos. 8:3; 9:3, 6, 15, 17; 10:6; 11:5; 12:9) would all happen according to the word of the Lord through Moses. Indeed, it all did happen. This threat of discipline permeated Hosea's message: virtually every chapter included some reference to God's punishment of the nation because of their sin.[7] Sin has consequences, and God's chosen are not exempt (see Amos 3:2). Sowing the wind reaps the whirlwind (Hos. 8:7); plowing wickedness reaps iniquity (Hos. 10:13). This principle is unchangeable, or God would be mocked (Gal. 6:7–8). God's love does not overlook sin nor does it not circumvent His justice; it operates within it. Even divine discipline is an act of His covenant love.

Although Hosea devotes much attention to the details of God's punishment, our concern here is not so much how God humbled the nation but that He did bring it low as evidence of His loyal love—as severe and as tough as it was. Keep Hosea 5:15 in mind: God punished them to awaken them to seek Him diligently. The curative nature of God's chastening hand evidenced in His dealings with wayward Israel relates to the church today as well. The church may not be subject to the same kind of calamities experienced by Israel, but Christians must remain conscious of the fact that their privileged position does not free them to sin and that God will—in fatherly love—discipline them as necessary with a view to holiness.

It would be foolish and unbiblical to assume that all the trials of life are demonstrations of God's chastening for sin. On the contrary, hard times are often the lot of the godliest of saints: Job proves that. However, we would be dishonest with ourselves and before the Lord if we claimed to be so sanctified that we never displeased Him (1 John 1:8, 10). You know your weaknesses, failures, and sins, and I know mine. The fact remains that the Lord does chasten His children as evidence of His love and concern for them (Heb. 12:5–11; see also Prov. 3:11–12). We, therefore, must be sensitive to what we may have done to displease Him and responsive to what He will do to correct us, to restore us to fellowship, and to promote within us more likeness to Christ. Hebrews 12:11 puts it all in proper perspective: "Now no chastening seems to be joyful for the present, but grievous; nevertheless, afterward it yields the peaceable fruit of righteousness to those who have been trained by it." Love can be tough, but let's be thankful that we are the objects of God's love and that He will evidence His love in the ways that are most needful for our spiritual development and good. And the happy truth is that God is always faithful to forgive us and to restore us to fellowship when we confess our sins, because "we have an Advocate with the Father, Jesus Christ the righteous" (1 John 1:9; 2:1). There is always a way back home. Don't misunderstand God's chastening hand.

THE DIRECTIONS

The Lord not only gives hope to wandering Israel by leaving the door to home open and doing what is necessary to make home attractive (the tough love); He provides the map with clear directions as to how to get there. If discipline was the evidence of God's loyal love and restoration its goal, then repentance was the proper response to it. Repentance was the way back home. Without repentance there could be no enjoyment or experience of reunion.

The directions for returning home were unmistakably clear: they could be ignored but could not be misunderstood. This is obvious from the root word used both for Israel's departure from the Lord and for their return to Him. The verbal root is *shwb*, which means to turn by reversing directions, by doing an about face. So whether the word designates apostasy or repentance depends on the direction headed—what's ahead and what's behind. So, on the one hand, Israel was bent on turning away from God (Hos. 11:7; literally, "hung up on apostasy"). God was behind them, and they were headed in the wrong direction. On the other hand, God instructed them to turn around and come back to Him (Hos. 6:1–3; 14:1–3). That is a particular focus of Hosea. Many of the other prophets instructed the people to turn around because judgment and destruction were in front of them; Hosea seemed to say to turn around because God was behind them—same result, different perspective. They were to do an about-face; they were to face the Lord and head directly home. The way back was straight and narrow, and there were no shortcuts.

Included in the general directions to turn around were specific signposts to mark the route even more clearly. The opening verses of Hosea 14 are most instructive in mapping the unmistakable waypoints of genuine repentance.

Reversing direction involved not only what should be done (a new course for life) but what should be said (a confession of faith). Hosea says, "Take words with you, and return to the LORD" and then proceeds to specify what the people were to say. The confession of faith is expressed with two petitions and two resolutions: four sets of words to mark their return to the Lord.

First were the words of confession: "Take away all iniquity" (Hos. 14:2). This petition admits guilt before the Lord and accepts blame before Him. When they were facing away from God, they were oblivious to sin and guilt: "They shall find in me no iniquity that is sin" (Hos. 12:8). How different it is when God is in view. When they turned around to face God, sensitivity to sin increased. The closer to God a person is, the more conscious that person becomes of sin. Sensitivity to sin necessarily and inevitably intensifies in view of God's holiness. That's the way it always is. Even what had been perceived as "little sins" are magnified in His presence, and the person becomes aware that those sins are the obstacles to enjoying God's presence. Confessing sins offers no excuses, but humbly pleas for divine forgiveness. Taking away guilt is what forgiveness is all about. It is essential to fellowship with God.

Second were words of commitment: "Receive us graciously" (Hos. 14:2) or more literally, "accept [the] good." This petition involves an offering to God of what He requires with the expectancy that He will receive what is offered.[8] A commitment of self in obedience is the essence of what God demands of His people. Micah summed up the good that God requires in these terms: doing justly, loving mercy, and walking humbly with God (Mic. 6:8; see also Deut. 10:12). The grace of divine forgiveness should generate the desire to please the Lord. This was Paul's logic when he said that those who live because of Christ's death and are thus the objects of God's love and forgiveness "should live no longer for themselves, but for Him who died for them and rose again" (2 Cor. 5:14–15). Similarly, the petition parallels Paul's admonition, in light of all the mercies of God which we have received, to present our bodies as "a living sacrifice, holy, acceptable to God, which is [our] reasonable service" (Rom. 12:1). The good life before God boils down to obedience, the way we show our love and gratitude (John 14:15). The amazing thing is that God is pleased with a life consecrated to Him.

Third were words of praise: "For we will offer the sacrifices of our lips" (Hos. 14:2), or more literally, "we will repay young bulls, our lips." The verb form "we will repay" is not merely a future tense but rather an expression of personal determination (a cohortative): "we resolve to repay." The verb itself is *shlm*, the root word for "peace," and it points to the votive or peace offerings, which were offered to the Lord in payment of a vow or in thanksgiving for salvation and grace. This, then, is a determined, personal resolution to render to the Lord what is owed and what He deserves because of His grace—praise and thanksgiving. The psalmist brings it all together: "You have loosed my bonds. I will offer to You the sacrifice of thanksgiving. . . . I will pay my vows to the Lord" (Ps. 116:16–18). The New Testament employs the same imagery, most likely with Hosea 14 in mind: "Therefore by Him let us continually offer the sacrifice of praise to God, that is, the fruit of our lips, giving thanks to His name" (Heb. 13:15). A believer at home with God will be full of praise, thanksgiving, and gratitude for grace. Praising the Lord is a sure sign that we are on the right path.

Fourth were words of dependence: "Assyria shall not save us. . . . For in You the fatherless finds mercy" (Hos. 14:3). Verse 3 expresses the forsaking of every empty hope—whether Assyria, horses, or idols. In stark contrast to all the things incapable of helping is the Lord, whose abundant mercy supplies the orphan's need. The orphan is a vivid example of one who is destitute and incapable of self-preservation, one who is completely dependent on another. The needy orphan represents the sense of helplessness that every repenter must have. Repentance involves abandonment to the mercies of God. The prophet Joel in one of the Bible's classic texts on repentance makes it clear that God is the penitent's hope: "Return to the LORD your God, for He is gracious and merciful, slow to anger, and of great kindness" (Joel 2:13). Confessing that there is no hope apart from God marks a step in the right direction. Indeed, it is an essential gospel truth.

The happy reality is that the Lord's invitation to repent is not ineffective. It is a spiritual law that God seeks a sinner with grace before the sinner seeks Him. Consequently, the directions He gives are certain to bring the sinner or the wanderer home; the path is clearly marked. Significantly, therefore, accompanying the invitation to return to the Lord was the assurance that the consequences of the tough love, designed to motivate repentance, would transition to tender love: "Come, and let us return to the LORD; for He has torn, but He will heal us; He has stricken, but He will bind us up" (Hos. 6:1). Similarly, the Lord reassured those who returned, "I will heal their backsliding [same word as Hos. 11:7], I will love them freely, for My anger has turned away from him" (Hos. 14:4). There is something wonderfully consistent about God's promise to forgive those who genuinely confess their sins. What Hosea assured his generation of is our guarantee, too: "If we confess our sins, He is faithful and just to forgive us our sins and to cleanse us from all unrighteousness" (1 John 1:9).

For every Christian troubled and disappointed with his level of spiritual experience and enjoyment, the closing words of Hosea are both encouraging and instructive: "Who is wise? Let him understand these things. Who is prudent? Let him know them. For the ways of the LORD are right; the righteous walk in them . . ." (Hos. 14:9). There is a way out of our predicament of spiritual dryness and dearth, a way to reverse a path littered with disobedience and sin. For those who are far from God, there is a way back. For those who are near the Lord, there is a way to be nearer still. The journey home is clear, and the reception home is guaranteed by the promise of God.

FOR FURTHER REFLECTION

1. Have you ever known a professing Christian who feels that he has lost out with God? How could you use the message of Hosea as an encouragement to him?
2. Think about where you would be were it not for the "buts" of God's grace in your life.
3. How has your knowing Christ changed your life?
4. When you do sin, why is it important to confess your sins before the Lord as soon as possible?

CONCLUSION

Christ is the central theme in the Bible. Although explicit statements about Him may not occur on every line and perhaps not even on every page, the message of Christ casts its shadow on the entire Scripture. Jesus Christ is God's final, perfect, and incomparable Word; indeed, in the final analysis, Jesus Christ is God's only Word for mankind. Every other biblical theme and topic in one way or another relates to Him and should be interpreted, understood, and applied in the light of Him. Not only is Christ the centerpiece in Scripture, but He is the glue and goal of time—both past and future. All history is ultimately redemptive, progressing with eternal purpose from sin's inception in Eden to sin's remedy on Calvary to sin's absence in glory. In eternity's covenant of redemption, God chose His Son to be the only Redeemer of His elect and promised to give His Son those elect people in consequence of His fulfilling all the covenant terms of redemption. From humanity's first need of a Savior, God gave His word that there would be a Savior. In the fullness of time, God sent His Son into the world of sinners to do all that a Savior needed to do to save His people from their sins. This is amazingly good news; it is the gospel. It is wonderfully in keeping with God's grace, then, that God has given the Scripture to reveal this Savior to needy sinners; without this special revelation to the world, there would be no hope.

Getting the message of the Bible, therefore, is paramount. The Bible points sinners to Christ, warns them against rejecting Christ, and guides believers to live in

Christ. Finding Christ—the gospel—is the key that both unlocks and locks in the message of the whole Word of God. This is true for the Old Testament as well as for the New Testament. It is the purpose of this series, The Gospel According to the Old Testament, to discover and to underline these remarkable truths particularly in the Old Testament, that portion of Scripture so often ignored or misunderstood by Christians. It has been the purpose of this study specifically to highlight those truths in Hosea.

Hosea lived and ministered over seven hundred years before the incarnation, and there were details about Jesus that he could not have known. He would not have known the specific incidents of Christ's earthly ministry or the mechanics of the Roman crucifixion by which Christ suffered and died. But Hosea in company with all his prophetic colleagues preached the gospel of salvation: "Of this salvation the prophets have inquired and searched diligently, who prophesied of the grace that would come to you, searching what, or what manner of time, the Spirit of Christ, who was in them was indicating when He testified beforehand the sufferings of Christ and the glories that would follow" (1 Peter 1:10–11). Hosea knew the gospel, and it is clear from the book that bears his name that he lived it and preached it passionately and powerfully to his generation.

Although Hosea's declaring the word of God—that is, speaking authoritatively in behalf of God—was the common and universal prophetic commission, how the Lord used the prophet himself to visualize the spoken message was unique. By divine command, Hosea's personal life became a living sermon of what he preached. Oddly enough, God's first command to Hosea was to get married, and then the Lord used that marriage to frame the message. The people were to look at Hosea's home life to learn something about God, grace, and the gospel. Because God inspired Hosea to record his experience and message as part of Scripture, we, too, can look and learn.

It has been my purpose in this little book to focus on those lessons. If you have picked up this book expecting an expositional commentary, you have been disappointed. Confessedly, the hardest thing about writing it has been to avoid addressing the specific details of interpretation. So much of Hosea's message begs for comment and explanation; there are some difficult statements. My concern was to put in focus the big picture that will ultimately help us understand the details and grasp the significance of Hosea's message. I want us to see that the book's subtitle, *The Gospel According to Hosea*, is not a stretch of words.

The book is small enough that a synopsis of each chapter at this point is not necessary, but just in case you're reading the conclusion first (which is not always a bad idea), I do want to outline my approach to the topic. In Part 1, I address essential facts about Hosea—who he was, when he lived, and what he believed. Too often in studying the Bible, people jump in looking for blessing and then wonder why they don't get it. The background data identify facts that are fundamental assumptions for properly interpreting the message. These three chapters discuss matters that must be factored into reading Hosea if we're going to see the gospel, not the least of which is Hosea's covenant theology that recognizes Christ at the core. Part 2 establishes the biblical basis for the symbolic significance of marriage and looks at Hosea's personal life as a model of God's relationship with His people. In the Bible, marriage is a choice symbol of God's relationship to His people. Hosea's relationship with Gomer, as tragic as it was, points to and highlights the beauty of Christ's relationship to His bride, the church. Hosea's life was full of the gospel. Part 3 sums up the main points of Hosea's sermon, which applies the tragedy of his own experience to God's relationship with Israel. The themes of divine love and covenant loyalty in contrast to Israel's sin uncover the heart of gospel grace. Looking at Hosea's life and "hearing" him preach justify his reputation for being the tenderest of the prophets, the prophet of grace and love.

Hosea links all this hope to the covenant of grace, the essence of which is Christ. To miss this about Hosea's message is to miss his point. God's gracious love, notwithstanding its sovereignty, is neither whimsical nor arbitrary. God's grace is experienced only in terms of Christ. God loves His Son, and He loves those who by covenant belong to His Son. The covenant union that believers have with Christ is ultimately the only explanation of God's acceptance of them. This is why the marriage symbolism that is an integral part of Hosea is so instructive regarding the gospel. As a father of two married sons, I have come to a new understanding and appreciation of the marriage bond. When my first son married, I experienced emotions that I did not know I was capable of. It is difficult to put into words the joy and satisfaction I felt toward my son's bride. Perhaps the strangest and newest thing for me was the total acceptance and love I have for his wife. Because of her oneness with my son, she is one with my family. So it is for my younger son and his bride. This whole business of having married sons has helped me understand a little of how our Heavenly Father views us as the bride of Christ. United to Christ, the Father loves us as He loves His Son and accepts us completely and unreservedly. In His great intercessory prayer for His people, the Lord Jesus said as much when He said to His Father, "You . . . have loved them as You have loved Me" (John 17:23). I can't think of anything more amazing than that.

In the light of our theological survey of Hosea's gospel, I want to suggest three lessons in conclusion. First, there should be a transparency in every Christian life that testifies to the power and grace of the gospel. Hosea provides a classic example: his life preached the gospel. So it should be for us all. Grace has transformed us from sinners to saints, has brought us out of darkness to light, and has raised us from spiritual death to spiritual life in Christ. Grace has made us new creations in Christ. This multifaceted spiritual transformation ought to be evident to those who see us, and it ought to open our mouths in testimony and praise. Second, there is hope for sinners because grace operates from the good pleasure of God's will, not because of personal merit or worth. Hosea loved Gomer in spite of what he knew about her; God loves us in spite of what He knows about us. There is no reason to despair of grace, because where sin abounds, grace abundantly abounds. Third, there is hope for Christians who have grown spiritually cold and have wandered away from the Lord that He is ready to forgive. Gomer hurt Hosea, but he took her back. Israel sinned heinously against the Lord, but He left the door open for their return. Backsliding Christians often convince themselves that the Lord is finished with them and that there is no way that He will forgive them again. Hosea's gospel shows the way back. Christians should never despair of grace.

It has been my desire and prayer from the beginning of this project that the Lord Jesus Christ would be evidently set forth and that the Holy Spirit would lead into truth by showing Christ and glorifying Him. Hosea provided ample means of achieving this desire. If this study has done anything to draw attention to Hosea's Savior, I give my humble thanks to the Lord.

APPENDIX

CHRIST OUT OF EGYPT: HOSEA 11:1 AND MATTHEW 2:15[1]

Matthew 2 records the search of the wise men for the newborn Christ. Having followed the special star to Jerusalem, they began asking for more specific directions. When Herod, the illegitimate usurper of the throne, heard about their search, he questioned the theologians in Jerusalem concerning the birthplace of Messiah. They knew right where to look, knowing Micah's prophecy that Bethlehem would be the birthplace of the promised King (Mic. 5:2). Herod learned from the wise men when the star had first appeared, and then he sent them on to Bethlehem, imploring them to return with the Messiah's address so he, too, could go and worship. Herod, of course, had other motives, and God warned the wise men to return to their homeland another way, avoiding Herod. After the wise men left, the Lord revealed to Joseph in a dream Herod's plot to kill Jesus and instructed him to take his family and escape to Egypt for safety. Before Matthew reveals the details of Herod's treachery in slaying all the children within the district and also before he records the actual return of Joseph and his family to Israel after Herod's death, Matthew sums up the whole episode by saying that they were in Egypt until the death of Herod.

> Now when they had departed, behold, an angel of the Lord appeared to Joseph in a dream, saying, "Arise, take the young Child and His mother, flee to Egypt, and stay there until I bring you word; for Herod will seek the young Child to destroy Him." When he arose, he took the young Child and His mother by night and departed for Egypt, and was there until the death of Herod, that it might be fulfilled which was spoken by the Lord through the prophet, saying, "Out of Egypt I called My Son." (Matt. 2:13–15)

It is in this summary statement before the account of the slaughter and return that Matthew refers to Hosea 11:1. We will see the importance of the placement of the text in due course.

At first glance, it seems that Matthew identifies Hosea's statement as one of the many Old Testament prophecies that were so precisely fulfilled in the Lord Jesus Christ. However, considering Hosea 11:1 in its context raises some questions about Matthew's hermeneutics. We could read this Old Testament text all day long and it would never cross our mind that it was directly prophesying Christ's infant flight to Egypt to escape Herod's murderous plot to destroy the promised Seed. Hosea is reviewing some Hebrew history and is without question alluding to God's gracious and loving exodus deliverance of Israel at their birth as a nation. Was Matthew just using his inspired imagination in applying this to Christ, or did he correctly recognize something beyond the surface in the statement that both God and Hosea intended? I suggest that Matthew correctly and astutely recognized the symbolic significance of

Hosea's exodus statement and artfully and justifiably applied it typically, or at least analogically, to Christ. In other words, Matthew is saying there is something about God's loving deliverance of Israel from Egypt that is analogous to God's loving protection of Christ from Herod. Rather than being guilty of taking Hosea's statement out of context and changing its intent, Matthew evidences a profound knowledge of the theology of the Old Testament generally and Hosea's theology specifically.

MATTHEW'S INTERPRETATION OF HOSEA

Matthew illustrates the importance of full context analysis, which includes attention to previously defined messianic clues. Without ignoring or violating the immediate context, he extends the analysis to the larger context of the book and ultimately to the larger context of the Testament. This is not the place to develop or review an extensive theological analysis of Hosea, but I will suggest a few things that Matthew apparently saw in Hosea's statement that warranted its application to this particular episode in the early life of Jesus.

First, he recognized the messianic significance of the exodus. This actual historic event marked the birth of Israel as a nation. However, the monumental deliverance from Egypt was more than an Independence Day occasion. It was a necessary progression in God's fulfilling His covenant promise to Abraham, at the heart of which was the promise of the Seed. God had told Abraham that his seed line of promise would be for four hundred years, not in the land of promise, but in a land that would afflict them and put them in servitude (Gen. 15:13–14). At the end of that predetermined period, "God remembered His covenant with Abraham, with Isaac, and with Jacob" and then set in motion through

Moses the promised judgment on Egypt and the liberation of the promised seed (Ex. 2:24). Although all this had obvious and immediate significance to those historical people, the ultimate significance of the exodus involved the preservation of the seed of promise with a divinely unrelenting view to the coming of the Seed of promise. As there had to be an Isaac before there could be the Christ, so there had to be a nation through whom Christ according to the flesh could come (Rom. 9:4–5). It is imperative to see the link between the seed and the Seed. The historical event of bringing Israel out of Egyptian bondage was a giant step toward the fullness of time. It was an epochal moment in the timeline of redemptive history.

Second, Matthew recognized the specific messianic significance of God's designation of Israel as "my son" (see also Ex. 4:22—"Israel is My son, My firstborn"). The title "son," like "seed," is one of those important clue words in the Old Testament that point to Christ.[2] Both words are theologically charged. Not only does the son reference speak of the unique relationship between God and those to whom the promise is given, but it also speaks of the ideal greater Son who is both the Seed and the Son of promise. By the time Hosea wrote, the expression "my son" had assumed even more explicit messianic significance in terms of God's covenant promise to David (2 Sam. 7:14—"I will be his Father, and he shall be My son"). It is imperative to see the link between *my son* and *my Son*. God's safeguarding His son Israel was an essential step toward the time when God would send and give His only begotten Son. Very simply said, in God's unfailing redemptive plan, there had to be an Israel if there were going to be a Christ.

Third, Matthew recognized the symbolic significance of Egypt and the exodus. What God did in delivering a visible Israel from a visible Egypt provided many specific object lessons illustrating what God always does for His people both spiritually and physically. Throughout the Old Testament, the inspired writers, from Moses to Malachi, used the exodus as a picture of God's gracious redemption, care, protection, and preservation of His people. The spiritual analogies are far too many to discuss at this point, but let me suggest a key point that is particularly relevant to Hosea's contextual argument and Matthew's perception. Because of Egypt's cruel oppression of Israel, Egypt became a vivid picture of bondage, persecution, and affliction in general. The goal of the Egyptian oppression is also theologically significant, and it therefore defined Egypt as more than merely a picture of indiscriminate oppression: the Egyptians attempted to destroy the promised Seed. Had Pharaoh's plan to kill all the sons of Israel succeeded, there would have been no Christ. The God-fearing midwives were the humble means by which God spared the male children and thereby secured the covenant promise. Consequently, Egypt was more than a place on the map. It was a picture of bondage and a symbol of that which was anti-God, anti-people of God, and ultimately anti-Christ. The exodus deliverance, accordingly, was a vivid picture of God's preserving His people and His promised Seed. Interestingly, Hosea illustrates this symbolic significance. Although Hosea 11:1 is a direct reference to geographical Egypt and the actual historical event of the exodus, the prophet elsewhere employed the term *Egypt* symbolically. For instance, in Hosea 9:3, as evident by the synonymously parallel lines, he identifies Egypt with Assyria: "But Ephraim shall return to Egypt, and shall eat unclean things in Assyria." Obviously, Assyria was not literally or geographically Egypt; it was acting like Egypt in that it was to become a place of oppression and bondage for the nation.

MATTHEW'S APPLICATION OF HOSEA

I think we can at least begin to see why Matthew said that Joseph's flight into Egypt with Jesus fulfilled Hosea's statement that God called His son out of Egypt. Rather than taking Hosea's statement out of context and infusing a new meaning into it, Matthew demonstrates a careful and thoughtful use of the text. He interpreted Hosea's statement not as the fulfillment of a singular word prediction but as the fulfillment of a picture prophecy, a type. He recognized an apparent point of correspondence between the historic exodus and Christ's protection from Herod.

Very much on the surface is the similarity in these incidents of divine intervention to deliver the designated "son" or "Son" from a life-threatening environment. Perhaps not as much on the surface, but nonetheless indisputable, is the integral continuity between preserving Israel and preserving the child Jesus. Both were necessary if the mediatorial work of the Man, Christ Jesus, was to be fulfilled. In a very real sense, Pharaoh and Herod had the same agenda: to eliminate the promised Seed. Pharaoh attempted to kill Christ's ancestors, which would have prevented His birth. Herod attempted to kill Christ after His birth, which would have prevented His saving work. I would dare say that Satan inspired them both in his vain efforts to devour the child not only as soon as He was born (Rev. 12:4) but also even long before He was born. Nothing, however, can frustrate or alter God's eternal purpose and promise concerning Christ: He delivered His Son from Egypt—both from Pharaoh's and from Herod's.

I believe that Matthew's placement of his quotation of Hosea 11:1 immediately after the proleptic statement of Herod's death (remember that prolepsis is a statement in anticipation of the reality it states) and before the recording of the actual events was a calculated irony and another evidence of his thorough knowledge of the type. As far as

Matthew was concerned, *Egypt* did not refer to geographical Egypt but to Herod's domain. Interpreting the type consistently required that Egypt be the place of oppression, not the place of refuge. The point of correspondence for the type is exhibited not in the geographical direction taken by Joseph and his family but in God's preservation of His Son.[3] Calling His Son out of Egypt was delivering His Son out of harm's way in Herod's Judea. Very simply stated, Christ's entrance into territorial Egypt was His escape from spiritual Egypt. John confirms that this is not a groundless analogy. He identified the place where the two eschatological witnesses would be slain because of opposition to the gospel as Sodom and Egypt, "where also our Lord was crucified" (Rev. 11:8). That was Jerusalem.

MATTHEW'S HERMENEUTICAL EXAMPLE

Much of the christological message of Hosea is revealed typically. The marriage motif is on the surface throughout the book, but it is not the only image the prophet uses to make a predictive point. I have often referred to these Old Testament types as picture prophecies. Although they are pictures, it is important to remember that they are divinely defined and consequently just as valid and authoritative as any directly verbal predictions made by the prophets. Types are not intended to obscure but to elucidate truth. By pointing to something in the real world, God expects us to understand something about the spiritual world. But sure enough, we have to think.

The New Testament unquestionably refers to and relies on the fulfillment of the Old Testament's picture prophecies. Not only does the New Testament give sufficient warrant for identifying types in the Old Testament, but it also establishes a model for interpreting types.[4] We ought, therefore, to learn from the New Testament writers and emulate them in our efforts to interpret the Old Testament. The New Testament often goes beyond the surface meaning, lifting a truth from its historic reference and applying its relevance to a new temporal setting; however, it never changes the truth.[5]

So while Matthew forthrightly declares the christological import of Hosea 11:1, he also illustrates two key principles required for us all when recognizing and interpreting types. First, he shows the importance of knowing the Scripture and how its parts integrate and work together to reveal God's redemptive scheme and purpose.[6] We must be sensitive to contextual clues. It is important to understand that being considerate of context means more than simply noting the verse before or the verse after. Consideration of context follows the pattern of the old ripple-ring illustration. Just as a stone thrown into a pond causes the ripples to move away from the center with increasing area, so must the context-sensitive interpreter move away from the text to its immediate context, to its book context, to its context in the particular Testament, and finally to its context in the whole of Scripture. I think that one reason so many do not see in Hosea 11:1 what Matthew saw is that they do not think past Hosea 11:2.

Second, Matthew shows the importance of sticking to the main message that links the type and the antitype. Keep it simple; there will usually be one main point of correspondence. Focus on the specific elements about the type that stand out in the context without trying to factor in everything that is conceivable. Remember that not even divinely inspired analogies are perfect parallels to the principal subject; they are not supposed to be lest the analogy (the type) satisfy the function of and replace the principal subject (the antitype). Matthew did not attempt to make a point-for-point correspondence between Israel's rescue from Pharaoh and Christ's escape from Herod; some things about the historic type did not apply to the future antitype, not the least of which was the direction traveled.

But what did correspond highlighted a beautiful gospel truth: God's purpose to redeem His people in Christ cannot fail. God guaranteed His covenant promise by assuring the coming of His Christ and the consequent accomplishing of the work of redemption. The exodus proved it; Hosea predicted it; Matthew reported it. Moses, Hosea, and Matthew all preached the same gospel.

NOTES

CHAPTER ONE: HOSEA: A MESSIANIC MAN

1 For a helpful discussion of the root *mshh*, see John N. Oswalt's contribution in *New International Dictionary of Old Testament Theology & Exegesis*, ed. William A. VanGemeren (Grand Rapids: Zondervan Publishing House, 1997), 2:1123–27.

2 J. B. Payne, for instance, says that "a 'messiah' was technically any man who had been consecrated to God's service by the application of holy anointing oil, which in turn symbolized the enabling presence of the Holy Spirit in his heart." *The Theology of the Older Testament* (Grand Rapids: Zondervan, 1972), 257–58. Similarly, Walter Kaiser remarks that "the oil of anointing, when used in worship, was a symbol of the divine Spirit; but in regal consecration it marked God's gift of His Spirit to aid the king of Israel in administering His rule." *Toward an Old Testament Theology* (Grand Rapids: Zondervan Publishing House, 1980), 148.

3 There are a couple of books on these other northern prophets that you should read: Raymond B. Dillard, *Faith in the Face of Apostasy: The Gospel According to Elijah & Elisha*, The Gospel According to the Old Testament (Phillipsburg, NJ: P&R Publishing, 1999) and Bryan D. Estelle, *Salvation Through Judgment and Mercy: The Gospel According to Jonah*, The Gospel According to the Old Testament (Phillipsburg, NJ: P&R Publishing, 2005).

4 For a brief analysis of the book's structure with helpful charts locating various themes in each section, see Robert D. Bell, "The Theology of Hosea," *Biblical Viewpoint* 30 (Nov. 1996): 37–44.

CHAPTER TWO: HOSEA: THE TIME OF HIS LIFE

1 Here is a list of Israel's kings:

- **Dynasty 1**
    - Jeroboam I, Nadab—23 years
- **Dynasty 2**
    - Baasha, Elah—25 years
    - Zimri—1 week
- **Dynasty 3**
    - Omri, Ahab, Ahaziah, Joram—45 years
- **Dynasty 4**
    - Jehu, Jehoahaz, Jehoash, Jeroboam II, Zechariah—89 years
    - Shallum—one month
- **Dynasty 5**
    - Menahem, Pekahiah—13 years
    - Pekah—20 years
    - Hoshea—9 years

2 For an explanation of Pekah's rival reign, see Edwin Thiele, *The Mysterious Numbers of the Hebrew Kings* (Grand Rapids: William B. Eerdmans Publishing, 1965), 123–25, and Walter C. Kaiser, *A History of Israel* (Nashville: Broadman & Holman Publishers, 1998), 361–62.

3 Relevant texts from the Assyrian records paralleling the biblical account can be found in James Pritchard, ed., *Ancient Near Eastern Texts* (Princeton: Princeton University Press, Third Edition, 1969), 283–84. Inscriptions from the time of Tiglath-pileser III specifically mention the plundering of Samaria, the annexation of the land of Naphtali to Assyria, the tribute exacted from Menahem, the disposition of Pekah, and the appointment of Hoshea along with a catalog of his tribute payments. It provides an interesting read.

CHAPTER THREE: HOSEA: HIS CREED

1 Douglas Stuart comments on Hosea's use of covenant theology: "Understanding the message of the book of Hosea depends upon understanding the Sinai covenant. The book contains a series of blessings and curses announced for Israel by God through Hosea. Each blessing or curse is based upon a corresponding type in the

Mosaic law. Some blessings and curses so specifically parallel the pentateuchal formulations that they border on 'citation'. . . . Although Hosea's style was in many ways original, his message was not at all innovative. Hosea's task was simply to warn that Yahweh intended to enforce the terms of his covenant." *Hosea-Jonah*, vol. 31 of *Word Biblical Commentary* (n.p.: Nelson Reference & Electronic, 1987), 6–7. Geerhardus Vos also suggests that the covenant between Israel and the Lord was central in Hosea's argument and sums up the covenant relationship under five heads: 1) "The union originated on the part of Jehovah"; 2) "The relationship had a definite historical beginning"; 3) "Though the union originated effectually on Jehovah's part, yet Israel was led freely to enter upon it"; 4) "Although the berith is thus traced back to its highest ideal source in the nature and choice of Jehovah, it nevertheless established a legally defined relationship"; 5) "The covenant is . . . a national '*berith*'." *Biblical Theology* (Grand Rapids: Wm. B. Eerdmans, 1948), 260–63.

2 For a more detailed analysis of each of the specific covenants, see my treatment in *Beginning at Moses: A Guide to Finding Christ in the Old Testament* (Greenville, SC: Ambassador-Emerald International, 2nd ed., 2001), 122–39.

3 Genesis 9:27 is difficult and subject to differing interpretations. I would offer this interpretative translation: "May God provide ample space for Japheth; may God take up residence in the tents of Shem; and may Canaan become God's servant." This suggests two significant truths about Messiah's identity. First, it names the descendants of Shem, the Semites, as the particular segment of the human race into which the Seed would come. Second, it suggests that it is God Himself who will come. The language of Noah is remarkably similar to that of John, who spoke of the eternal Word's becoming flesh and dwelling among men (John 1:14). For a similar analysis, see Walter C. Kaiser Jr., *Toward an Old Testament Theology* (Grand Rapids: Zondervan, 1980), 81–82.

4 For a general discussion of some of the Mosaic shadows, see *Beginning at Moses*, 270–93 and Tremper Longman III, *Immanuel in Our Place: Seeing Christ in Israel's Worship*, The Gospel According to the Old Testament (Phillipsburg, NJ: P&R Publishing, 2001).

CHAPTER FOUR: A MARRIAGE PORTRAIT

1 I refer to Genesis 2 as the anthropological and covenant account of creation because of its summary dismissal of the details of creation (2:4) and its fixed focus on man's creation (2:7), his paradise home (2:8–14), his uniqueness among all the creatures (2:20), his incompleteness apart from woman (2:18), and the covenant terms for his avoiding death (2:16–17).

2 The verb "I will make" (*'e'eseh*) is a cohortative, a verbal form used to express strong personal interest, determination, and resolve.

3 In view of the confession's statement, I should explain my reference to God's passion. In describing the one true and living God, the Westminster Confession of Faith says that God is "a most pure spirit, invisible, without body, parts, or passions . . . immutable . . . incomprehensible . . ." (2.1). That God is incomprehensible stands over every description of His being and perfections. Comprehending pure spirit is impossible. So God through the grace and condescension of His self-revelation speaks in terms that man can understand. God has no body, yet the Scripture speaks of His hand or arm or eyes. We call these *anthropomorphisms*: terms of human form that reveal something about God. These are figures of speech whose point of similarity is in function rather than shape. So, for instance, that God has eyes declares that God sees. Likewise, God is without passion, yet the Scripture often attributes emotions to Him, such as jealousy. We call these *anthropopathisms*: terms of human emotion that reveal something about God. God is a person, and feeling is part of personality. But herein is an essential difference between God and man and why the confession says that God is without passion. Our emotions tend to be determined by things outside of ourselves and are subject to constant change. We can be happy one moment and sad the next, depending on the attendant circumstances. But God is immutable—not subject to change—and independent—unaffected by anything outside of Himself. God never reacts. As the *Westminster Confession* says, He is "independent upon the creature, so as nothing is to Him contingent, or uncertain" (2.2). So the infinite and immutable "feelings" inherent to the divine nature are not to be understood as varying emotions. But without refer-

ring to them in terms of human emotions, I suppose we could never understand anything about them.

4 Although recognizing that he employs more sermonic eloquence and rhetoric than exegetical evidence, I can't help but love the way C. H. Spurgeon states the messianic focus of this psalm in *The Treasury of David* (Grand Rapids: Zondervan, 1977), I:315. "Some here see Solomon and Pharaoh's daughter only—they are short-sighted; others see both Solomon and Christ—they are cross-eyed; well-focused spiritual eyes see here Jesus only, or if Solomon be present at all, it must be like those hazy shadows of passers-by which cross the face of the camera, and therefore are dimly traceable upon a photographic landscape. 'The King,' the God whose throne is for ever and ever, is no mere mortal and his everlasting dominion is not bounded by Lebanon and Egypt's river. This is no wedding song of earthly nuptials, but an Epithalamium for the Heavenly Bridegroom and his elect spouse."

5 Simon J. Kistemaker, also recognizing Hebrew betrothal customs in this text, offers a helpful summary and draws the lines to the spiritual significance in *Revelation*, New Testament Commentary (Grand Rapids: Baker, 2001), 514.

6 Charles Hodge, *Commentary on the First Epistle to the Corinthians* (Grand Rapids: Eerdmans, 1965), 112.

CHAPTER FIVE: UP CLOSE AND PERSONAL

1 Douglas Stuart is correct that a reconstruction of Hosea's personal life is impossible from the data of Hosea 1–3. He says, "We are told only such details as happen to serve metaphorical/typological purposes. The focus of the early chapters is not on Hosea and his family but on God and Israel." *Hosea-Jonah*, vol. 31 of *Word Biblical Commentary* (n.p.: Nelson Reference & Electronic, 1987), 12. I agree that the principal focus is on God and Israel, but I would suggest that enough about Hosea's personal experience is recorded to make his life a vivid object lesson of the spiritual message.

2 For more reading on the different interpretations of the marriage, see the following: Gleason L. Archer, *A Survey of Old Testament Introduction* (Chicago: Moody Press, Revised and Expanded, 1994), 357–59; C. Hassell Bullock, *An Introduction to the Old Testament*

Prophetic Books (Chicago: Moody Press, 1986), 88–91; Hobart E. Freeman, *An Introduction to the Old Testament Prophets* (Chicago: Moody Press, 1968), 178–82; Leon Wood, *The Prophets of Israel* (Grand Rapids: Baker Book House, 1979), 278–80.

3 Tremper Longman III and Raymond B. Dillard, *An Introduction to the Old Testament* (Grand Rapids: Zondervan Publishing House, 2nd ed., 2006), 403. Geerhardus Vos comes to the same conclusion: "The dispute between the allegorists and realists is interesting, but doctrinally the points of arrival on each view coincide," in *Biblical Theology* (Grand Rapids: Wm. B. Eerdmans Publishing Co., 1948), 261.

4 John Calvin, *Commentaries on the Twelve Minor Prophets* (Grand Rapids: Baker Books, reprint 1999), 1:44.

5 Edward J. Young, *An Introduction to the Old Testament* (Grand Rapids: Wm. B. Eerdmans Publishing Co., 1949), 245–46.

6 C. F. Keil, *The Twelve Minor Prophets*, trans. James Martin (Grand Rapids: Wm. B. Eerdmans Publishing Co., 1967), 1:35.

7 Calvin, 45.

8 Young, 246.

9 Keil, 36.

10 Even a proponent of the symbolic view admits, "There is much to be said in defense of this literal interpretation. For one thing, the prophecy reads as straightforward narrative. At first sight, we receive the impression that these things are to be understood as actually having taken place." Young, 245.

11 J. Barton Payne, a proponent of the harlot view, says, "The point is that God in His wisdom saw fit to overrule His usual standard that would have prohibited the marriage of His servant to an ungodly partner . . . for the sake of revelation. The very enormity of Hosea's situation is what drives home the theme of God's undivorceable concern for the unworthy. . . ." *Encyclopedia of Biblical Prophecy* (New York: Harper and Row, Publishers, 1973), 394.

12 This is essentially the notion of Douglas Stuart (11–12). He explains that Gomer's identification as a " 'prostituting' woman in 1:2 cannot be taken as a literal statement of her profession or practice. She is merely an Israelite—all of whom are 'prostitutes' as the verse implies, that is, all of whom have broken Yahweh's covenant."

13 Gleason Archer's concluding remarks regarding the Gomer problem represent the proleptic view, even addressing its principal weakness of accounting for the precise wording of God's command to Hosea. "The better solution to this problem is to be found in the supposition that at the time Hosea married Gomer, she was not a woman of overtly loose morals. If Hosea delivered his message in later years, he may have looked back upon his own domestic tragedy and seen in it the guiding hand of God. Hence the Lord's encouragement to him to marry her in the first place, though her future infidelity was foreknown to God, would have been tantamount to a command: 'Go, marry an adulterous woman,' even if the command did not come to the prophet in precisely these words." *A Survey of Old Testament Introduction*, 359.

14 Ludwig Koehler and Walter Baumgartner define the word at Hosea 1:2 as "inclined to fornicate" in *The Hebrew and Aramaic Lexicon of the Old Testament*, trans. and ed. M. E. J. Richardson (Leiden: Brill, 2001), 1:276.

15 That Gomer was a child of her times is the principal point according to Douglas Stuart (34): "Because Hosea's wife and children will be Israelites, they will automatically be exposed to and entangled by . . . 'prostitution,' syncretism/disloyalty to Yahweh. The presumption of the passage is that any Israelite woman Hosea married and any children he had would automatically be tainted by this 'prostitution,' so great was Israel's corruption and religious unfaithfulness at the time."

16 This notion is suggested by the Hebrew grammar. One of the functions of the Piel is to express iterative or repetitive action, and the active participle often designates habitual action. Thus, I say that she was enslaved in the adulterous behavior.

17 Some interpreters, however, do contend that Hosea's marrying Gomer included a ready-made family. McComiskey, a proponent of the harlot view, argues that Hosea adopted the children: "According to the view set forth here, Yahweh commanded Hosea not only to marry a woman of ill-repute, but to adopt the children born to her as a result of her promiscuous relationships. This view construes the first genitive in the double-duty construction . . . as a characteristic genitive, and the second genitive as source." Thomas

McComiskey, "Hosea," in vol. 1 of *The Minor Prophets: An Exegetical & Expository Commentary*, ed. Thomas Edward McComiskey (Grand Rapids: Baker Book House, 1992), 15.

18 For convincing arguments that the woman is Gomer, see McComiskey, 50 and Leon J. Wood, "Hosea" in vol. 7 of *The Expositor's Bible Commentary*, ed. Frank E. Gæbelein (Grand Rapids: Zondervan Publishing House, 1985), 182. Stuart (11), on the other hand, opines, "Since it cannot be proved that Gomer is the same wife described in chap. 3, nothing about Gomer's marital fidelity can be learned." He further suggests that Hosea married a second wife, presumably after Gomer's death, 12.

19 For a similar explanation of the verb construction, see McComiskey, 20–21 and Robert B. Chisholm Jr., *Handbook on the Prophets* (Grand Rapids: Baker Academic, 2002), 339–340.

CHAPTER SIX: THE GRACIOUS COVENANT

1 Perhaps a little digression is in order to explain what I mean by new covenant idealism. Jeremiah 31:31–34 is the only Old Testament passage that employs the term *new covenant*, but its essence is a common prophetic theme (see, for instance, Isa. 24, 55, 61; Ezek. 34, 37). Like the Mosaic covenant, the new covenant does not so much advance knowledge about the person of Messiah as it does the benefits and application of His work. Throughout his message, Jeremiah had explained God's judgment on Judah in terms of their breach of the covenant. It is significant that he proclaims God's gracious salvation of a future generation of Israel in terms of covenant renewal. Although Hosea does not employ the yet-to-be terminology "coined" by Jeremiah, I believe he refers to the same realization of God's covenant grace resulting in regeneration (a change of heart), reconciliation (a change in relationship with God), and pardon (a change in legal standing, or justification). Significantly, the New Testament clearly expresses that this new covenant is not uniquely for Israel. Various New Testament texts allude to the new covenant, and Hebrews 8:8–12 and 10:16–19 quote the passage completely. The New Testament makes it clear that the personal benefits of the new covenant are applied to every individual believer of the gospel.

2 Although I will not discuss the issues fully, I will remark on my historic/covenant premillennial perspective that comes out of my rather literalistic approach to Jeremiah's description of the new covenant. It seems to me from Jeremiah that a day is coming in which God will apply these saving benefits to the nation of Israel as a whole; there is going to be a universal knowledge and acceptance of the covenant. That has never happened before; it has not happened yet. Other Old Testament passages reveal that Gentiles are included in that glorious day, but Jeremiah's special focus is on Israel (see, for instance, Amos 9:11–12; Zech. 8:22–23). Zechariah spoke of a day when God "will pour on the house of David and on the inhabitants of Jerusalem the Spirit of grace and of supplication; then they will look on Me whom they have pierced . . ." (Zech. 12:10). God will send His Spirit to administer saving grace, regenerating the people and causing them to call upon the Lord as they look in faith to the Messiah, who so many years earlier had died for them. I believe that this is what Paul refers to when he says that all Israel will be saved. Interestingly, he explains that coming salvation in terms of Jeremiah's new covenant prophecy: "For this is My covenant unto them, when I shall take away their sins" (Rom. 11:27; compare this with Jer. 31:34). I believe that this national conversion will occur as one of the great attendant acts of the second coming of the Lord Jesus. Although the nation as a whole will be saved, it is important to note that the grace of the new covenant is applied individually to the hearts of the people. Nowhere does Scripture ever hint that people are saved by virtue of nationality. Even the physical seed of Abraham can become the spiritual seed only by exercising the same faith as did Abraham himself.

3 For an extremely helpful verse-by-verse commentary, I would recommend Thomas McComiskey, "Hosea," in vol. 1 of *The Minor Prophets: An Exegetical & Expository Commentary*, ed. Thomas Edward McComiskey (Grand Rapids: Baker Book House, 1992). See also Douglas Stuart, *Hosea-Jonah*, vol. 31 of *Word Biblical Commentary* (n.p.: Nelson Reference & Electronic, 1987). For a concise section-by-section summary see Robert B. Chisholm Jr., *Handbook on the Prophets* (Grand Rapids: Baker Academic, 2002), 335–68.

4 Admittedly, there is some degree of speculation regarding what and how much Hosea or any other prophet personally understood. I would concur with Kaiser that the prophets knew what they wrote about. Kaiser sums it up this way in his comments on 1 Peter 1:10–12. "There are five things the prophets were certain of when they wrote their texts. They knew they were predicting that: (1) the Messiah would come; (2) the Messiah would suffer; (3) the Messiah would be glorified (in kingly splendor); (4) the order of events 2 and 3 was that the suffering came first, and then the glorious period followed; and (5) his message had been revealed to the prophets not only for their own day, but also for a future generation. . . ." He continues, "Nevertheless, the writers can and do have an *adequate* understanding of the subject on which they write even if it is not a *comprehensive* control of all the particulars and parts that belong to that subject." Walter C. Kaiser, Jr., *The Uses of the Old Testament in the New* (Chicago: Moody Press, 1985), 20–21.

5 William L. Holladay, *A Concise Hebrew and Aramaic Lexicon of the Old Testament* (Grand Rapids: William B. Eerdmans Publishing Company, 1971), 228.

6 Geerhardus Vos in *Biblical Theology* (Grand Rapids: Wm. B. Eerdmans Publishing Company, 1948) recognizes the importance of the exodus and its revelation of God's redemptive purposes. He says that "the Exodus from Egypt is the Old Testament redemption" and bases that statement on "the inner coherence of Old Testament and New Testament religion" (109). Claiming that both Testaments share the "realism of redemption," he says, "The substance upon which the impression was made under the Old Testament may have been earthly clay; none the less the matrix that stamped it bore the lineaments of eternal law and truth" (109). He then offers a most helpful discussion of what he calls "the outstanding principles of the exodus-deliverance that were thus made regulative of all future salvation" (110–21). Some of those principles are highlighted in the following discussion.

7 Allan P. Brown suggests that God in the role of husband gave gifts to His bride as tangible evidence of His electing love, including the law and the land. "The Theology of Hosea" (PhD diss., Bob Jones University, 1975), 304.

8 This statistic comes from Robert D. Bell, "The Theology of Hosea," *Biblical Viewpoint* 30 (Nov. 1996): 37–44. This article offers a helpful analysis of the structure of Hosea's prophecy, identifying twenty-four sections, and includes several concise tables reflecting repetitive terms and themes: names of God, nations, sins, punishments, and God's kindness.

9 For a more in-depth discussion of the significance of this divine name, see my treatment in *The Beauty of Holiness: A Guide to Biblical Worship* (Greenville, SC: Ambassador-Emerald International, 2006), 62–64; 253–57.

10 There is a general consensus regarding the covenant implications of the name *Yahweh*. Robert Reymond says that "God in his Yahwistic character is the self-existent, self-determining, faithful God of the covenant" in *A New Systematic Theology of the Christian Faith* (Nashville: Thomas Nelson, 1998), 158. J. Barton Payne claims, "'Yahweh' ('faithful presence') is God's testamental nature, or name," in *The Theology of the Older Testament* (Grand Rapids: Zondervan Publishing House, 1972), 148. Similarly, John Howard Raven, a Reformed and conservative scholar of the late nineteenth and early twentieth centuries, concluded that *Jehovah* is "preeminently the covenant name of God." He continues, "The God who reveals himself to each succeeding generation as each generation has need and as each generation is able to receive the revelation, is the God who can never fail to keep every promise he has made." *The History of the Religion of Israel: An Old Testament Theology* (Grand Rapids: Baker Book House, 1979, reprint from 1933 edition), 48.

11 Bell, 40.

CHAPTER SEVEN: THE BROKEN COVENANT: THE BRIGHT SIDE

1 L. Berkhof devotes an entire chapter to dealing with what he calls the dual aspect of the covenant. His concluding section explaining the existence of the unregenerate in the covenant is most helpful. He delineates the following: (1) "They are in the covenant as far as their responsibility is concerned"; (2) "They are in the covenant in the sense that they may lay claim to the promises

which God gave when He established His covenant with believers and their seed"; (3) They are in the covenant in the sense that they are subject to the ministrations of the covenant"; (4) They are in the covenant also as far as the common covenant blessings are concerned." He then concludes, "It should be noted that, while the covenant is an eternal and inviolable covenant, which God never nullifies, it is possible for those who are in the covenant to break it. If one who stands in the legal covenant relationship does not enter upon the covenant of life, he is nevertheless regarded as a member of the covenant. His failure to meet the requirements of the covenant involves guilt and constitutes him a covenant breaker. . . . This explains how there may be, not merely a temporary, but a final breaking of the covenant, though there is no falling away of the saints." *Systematic Theology* (Grand Rapids: Wm. B. Eerdmans Publishing Co., 1941), 289.

2 Geerhardus Vos concurs that the "covenant is, according to Hosea, as it is to all New Testament writers, a national 'berith'" in *Biblical Theology* (Grand Rapids: Wm. B. Eerdmans Publishing Co., 1948), 262.

CHAPTER EIGHT: THE BROKEN COVENANT: THE DARK SIDE

1 Walter C. Kaiser, *Toward an Old Testament Theology* (Grand Rapids: Zondervan, 1978), 199.

2 John Howard Raven defines *khesedh* more broadly: "It is a characteristic word in Hosea, who uses it to express the natural attitude of Jehovah to his people, and man's natural attitude to his fellow-man, as the reflection of that love (2:19; 4:1; 6:4, 6; 10:12; 12:6)." *The History of the Religion of Israel: An Old Testament Theology* (Grand Rapids: Baker Book House, reprint ed., 1979), 340–41.

3 Walter C. Kaiser also recognizes this dual aspect of this charge of ignorance: "Usually the expression 'knowledge of God' meant theology or doctrine; what Israel lacked was respect for the law of God. . . . But it also meant a personal experience . . . and relationship with the only true God." *Toward an Old Testament Theology* (Grand Rapids: Zondervan, 1978), 199. Raven, however, while acknowledging that the "fundamental error of Israel

was that they did not know Jehovah," argues that the experimental sense of knowledge is primarily in view: "Since Hosea gained his deep knowledge of God by his own tragic experience, he came to realize that true knowledge of God can be gained in no other way. It is in this experimental sense that we should understand his frequent references to the knowledge of God" (334).

4 One of the tables that Robert D. Bell includes in his theme analysis of Hosea identifies the sin passages throughout the prophecy in three categories: idolatry, moral corruption, and political alliance. "The Theology of Hosea," *Biblical Viewpoint* 30 (Nov. 1996): 42.

5 The construction *zanoh* (infinitive absolute) *thizneh* (imperfect) puts the accent on the certainty of the event: "the land has certainly committed fornication."

CHAPTER NINE: THE WAY BACK HOME

1 Allan Brown offers a similar analysis of God's threefold plan to restore His people in "The Theology of Hosea" (PhD diss., Bob Jones University, 1975), 117–120.

2 For a general discussion regarding the gospel and christological content of the Old Testament sacrifices, see my treatment in *Beginning at Moses: A Guide to Finding Christ in the Old Testament* (Greenville, SC: Ambassador-Emerald International, 2nd ed., 2001) and Tremper Longman III, *Immanuel in Our Place: Seeing Christ in Israel's Worship*, The Gospel According to the Old Testament (Phillipsburg, NJ: P&R Publishing, 2001).

3 McComiskey concurs: "This affirmation that God will increase the numbers of his people beyond counting not only assures God's loyalty to his promise and to his people, but it envisions the inclusion of countless numbers of Gentiles in the promise as well." "Hosea," in vol. 1 of *The Minor Prophets: An Exegetical & Expository Commentary*, ed. Thomas Edward McComiskey (Grand Rapids: Baker, 1992), 29.

4 See the Appendix for the messianic significance of Hosea 11:1.

5 McComiskey, although not with my dogmatism, recognizes the possible messianic identification: "Hosea does not identify this leader, and the statements may simply be an affirmation of unity with no

particular individual intended, or it may refer to Yahweh or to the messianic King." Ibid.

6 For a discussion of christophanies including the Angel of the Lord, see *Beginning at Moses*, 145–63.

7 For all the specific references, consult again the helpful chart in Robert D. Bell, "The Theology of Hosea," *Biblical Viewpoint* 30 (Nov. 1996): 43.

8 McComiskey remarks that good "stands for that which is worthy of divine acceptation" (229).

APPENDIX: CHRIST OUT OF EGYPT: HOSEA 11:1 AND MATTHEW 2:15

1 This appendix is an adaptation from my book *Beginning at Moses: A Guide to Finding Christ in the Old Testament* (Greenville, SC: Ambassador-Emerald International, 2nd ed., 2001), 256–61. For a similar explanation of Matthew's use of Hosea, see Walter C. Kaiser Jr., *The Uses of the Old Testament in the New* (Chicago: Moody Press, 1985), 47–53.

2 Kaiser, 49, defends this notion of a special sense for the word "son": "It is in the deliberate application of what had become by now a technical title, 'My Son,' that the correlation between Hosea 11:1 and Matthew 2:15 begins to become most direct." He continues, "This designation, 'My Son,' became a technical term and an appellation that could be applied either collectively to the nation as the object of God's love and election or specifically to that final representative person who was to come in Christ."

3 Kaiser states the same: "The fact that Matthew introduced this quote at verse 15 and not after verse 20 or even verse 22 clearly points to the fact that the *Exodus*, or *departure*, of the Holy Family from Egypt is *not* the reason for introducing the quotation at this point. Instead, the emphasis falls exactly where it did in the context of Hosea: the preserving love of God for his seed, Israel" (51).

4 Sidney Greidanus says that "Especially because the New Testament writers believe that Jesus has ushered in the messianic age, they see God's past acts of redemption as shadows, prefigurations, and types of the new age that has dawned in Christ." He goes on to conclude: "We are, however, able to discern in the New Testament

a way of typology that is more disciplined and that can also be used today as a bridge from the Old Testament to Christ in the New Testament." *Preaching Christ from the Old Testament: A Contemporary Hermeneutical Method* (Grand Rapids: William B. Eerdmans, 1999), 213, 215.

5 Kaiser forthrightly claims that this messianic application was well within the scope of Hosea's intent: "This is biblical typology at its best, for it begins with a clear designation, is limited in its sphere of operation to the act of preservation and deliverance, and is circumscribed in its effects: the redemptive action of God is history. There is no distortion or abuse of the context of Hosea by Matthew; nor has he added his own interpretation to the text" (53).

6 Greidanus makes a key point about discerning types. "As promise-fulfillment functions within redemptive history because God makes and fulfills his promises in redemptive history, so typology functions within redemptive history because God acts in redemptive history in regular patterns. God accomplishes his redemptive plan not only progressively from promise to fulfillment but also uniformly through similarity of redemptive acts." He notes further, "the major presupposition underlying typological interpretation is that God as Lord of history works out his redemptive plan in history. . . . Faith in God's providence is the indispensable foundation of typological interpretation" (212–13).

INDEX OF SCRIPTURE